I0161044

FARMLAND

NEW METHODIST CHURCH

CIVIL BEND

THE GENERAL STORE

OLD SCHOOL HOUSE

THE BARN

#10

#11

#3

#17

THE HOME PLACE

#14

FARMLAND

N

#15

1 OLD METHODIST CHURCH
2 CENTRAL PHONE OFFICE
3 CELLAR
4 PEACH TREES
5 GRAPES
6 BLACKBERRY PATCH
7 WELL FOR HOUSE
8 GARDEN
9 ASPARAGUS PATCH
10 WALNUT GROVE
11 OUTHOUSE
12 APRICOT TREES
13 WELL FOR ANIMALS
14 BILL HIGHTREE HOUSE
15 UNCLE HARVEY'S
16 PASTURE
17 GARAGE
18 BROODER HOUSE
19 TOMATO PATCH

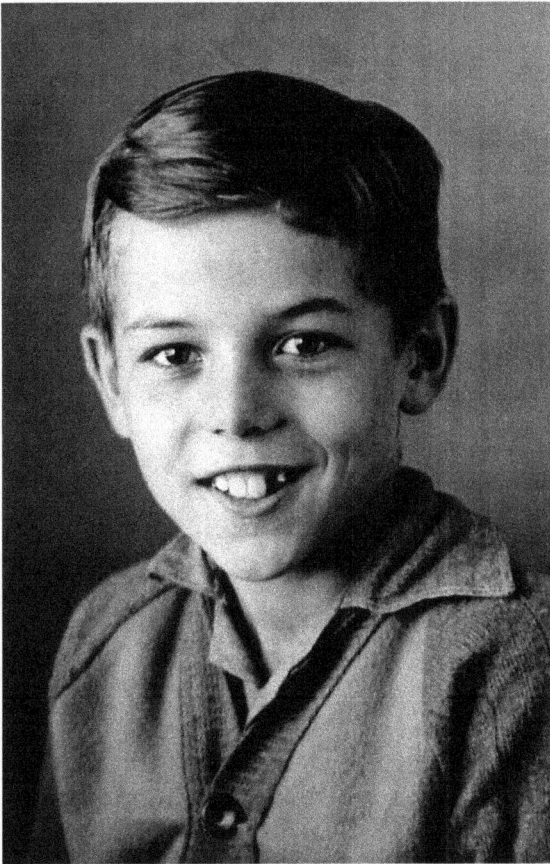

Stories of Civil Bend
By Lee Roy Bruner

ROSE OF SHARON
PRESS
LOS ANGELES

Stories of Civil Bend © 2019 by Lee Roy Bruner

Edited by Michael Lane Bruner

Photo on the title page is of the author, Lee Roy Bruner, at age 8.

ISBN: 978-1-937073-94-7 (Paperback)
978-1-937073-93-0 (Hardcover)

"The one thing that you have that nobody else has is you. Your voice, your mind, your story, your vision. So write and draw and build and play and dance and live as only you can."

Neil Gaiman

"Write your own story."

Anonymous

ACKNOWLEDGEMENTS

The author thanks the following individuals for their kind assistance in the production of this book of memories: Stephen Bruner, Sharon Redd, Debbie Hemenway, Penny Bruner-Scroggs, Dorothy Mae Fisher-Bruner, Vivian Bruner, Linda and Alan Goodwin, Carol Krepel, Mina Dishman, Charline Harris, Pam Bruner, Dick Means, and S.A. Griffin. Any errors remain my own.

CONTENTS

GROWING UP RIGHT

I will go on record and repeat what many have said across the years: "I wouldn't trade my life for yours or any other." We are all born into a time and place for a reason. The life we live is nothing more than the sum total of the choices we make from our circumstances. Life's challenges are opportunities to become who we want to become. Most of you about to read my *Stories of Civil Bend* have no idea how great you have it, and when you get to be my age I hope you will have that realization.

I love life because God gives us free choice, which is the greatest gift next to life itself. I like to think most of my choices in life have been good ones, but once in a while we all make bad choices. That is how we learn, for deep within us is a voice that admonishes us when we make bad choices, which I call the whispers of life.

LIFE

I can't remember this early morn,
The price you pay for being born.
I've forgotten, I can't remember.
What happened since last December?
It's spring again!

This body of mine, oh how tender,
Reminds me of a young tree in the timber.
Don't hurt me. Only so much can I bend,
Even though, young limbs can easily mend.
Young hearts and spirits, how easily they break.
Loving, tender care is what they take.
It's beautiful here!

Summer awakens the life in me.
God said, this is the way it would be.
See the flowers and weeds, how they grow?
It is true, you reap what you sow.
So many firsts this time of year.
Please stop, look, smell and hear.
Will I remember this? We go through time so fast!

Fall, autumn, call it what you may.
Is this the best time of day?
Am I wiser? Do I understand my brother?
Is the secret of life to love one another?
Serious times in my mind right now.
Am I finally learning, where, when, why and how?
Life is really great!

Winter is a graceful, slower pace.
Time to think and review the race.
This test was better than I ever thought.
No greater purchase could be bought.
My body weakens, every move is slow.
Is that the sunshine I see through the snow?
It will soon be spring again!

In listening to those whispers over time, I have come to appreciate the great freedom I enjoyed growing up as a child, living on a secluded family farm. To try and characterize that freedom, let me relate just a few of the experiences I had, and memories I have, simply because I was born at this time and place, in this protected world.

How fortunate I was, from the time I can remember, to have lived in a small, remote, and very safe place in northwest Missouri, in a now lost farmhouse, near a now lost village called Civil Bend, near a now lost farming town called Pattonsburg.

When I was a child, Civil Bend was an inland farming village with a population of about fifty or less, and anyone traveling on Highway 69 from Kansas City, Missouri to Des Moines, Iowa would pass a sign that read Civil Bend two miles to the right, but who would ever turn off to see that town?

Our house was an additional mile past Civil Bend to the east. If you drew a circle with a diameter of two miles, and if you drew Civil Bend in the middle, then you would have a circle of my world. Probably everybody living in that circle knew who the Bruners were. As for myself as a young child, I knew only a few of my fellow citizens. If I did know them, say as classmates in school, I didn't know where most of them lived.

So why did I write these stories about growing up in an isolated Missouri farming village during the Great Depression, World War II, and the years just after? Well, let me tell you.

It's all about growing up right.

The memories I relate of my experiences in Civil Bend from the 1930s to the 1950s begin about the age of four and continue until I left home, right after high school. These are true stories of a way of life lost in time. They are stories that go from tragic depths to comic heights. They are stories of winning and losing and learning life's lessons.

The orchards I walked in, the schools I attended, the General Store where my family traded, the house I was raised in, and the church I attended every Sunday unless I was sick are all gone. The town of Civil Bend is also gone: destroyed to make way for an interstate highway. Even the town of Pattonsburg, where I attended high school and spent my weekends as a teenager, was burned to the ground for dramatic effect in a Hollywood movie.

I hope therefore that you, the kind and patient reader, can somehow catch the feeling and the magic of a time and place, and a way of life, truly gone forever.

The farmhouse I was raised in and the General Store in Civil Bend were about a mile apart, and I walked that road untold times as a young boy with a penny in my pocket to purchase a candy bar. Sometimes folks would stop their car and ask where I was going. I would say, "I'm going to the General Store!" The driver might then say, "Well hop on the running board and hang on tight!" I would then put my arm around the post dividing the front and rear window, the driver would take off, and I would feel like Superman, my feet off the ground as if I was flying.

We were probably going twenty miles per hour.

They would stop at my destination, and I would first go to the Central Office to chat with Bertie and Frank Brown, who managed the local phone system, and to play with their dog. Bertie might give me a piece of hard ribbon candy or even a cookie if I got lucky. I would then walk confidently and happily across the street to the General Store and visit a few elderly men I called the Spit and Whittle Gang who were always sitting there on benches. These were retired fellows who chewed tobacco, spat in a copper pot, seldom missing, and were always carving away on a piece of wood making something or other. They always greeted me with a smile, calling me by name: "Well, here comes Lee Roy Bruner himself!"

After suitable conversation, I would go into the General Store to make my purchase. Chrisy Reno, the owner, knowing I had my penny, would ask if I wanted a Baby Ruth or a Butterfinger candy bar. I would make my decision, pay for it with my penny, put the candy safely in my pocket, and then mosey for a while around the store. They had everything in there from clothes to groceries, plus all kinds of toys and bulk cookies. Chrisy knew my Dad, and he knew all of my fourteen brothers and sisters, and he knew we would never steal anything, so he would always leave me be. After about fifteen minutes of browsing I would tell him goodbye and head home, munching my candy bar, making it last as long as I could.

I write you this opening story and the ones that follow because I want you to imagine you are me as a young child in Civil Bend, and I am the friendly driver stopping to offer you a lift. You happily accept, knowing where you are hoping to go, and knowing you are more than welcome there, and I say, "Here, have an ice cold Whistle Pop soda, and I will take you down the road a piece you might find interesting. Hop on the running board and hold on tight!" And I hope you will feel like you are flying, for we are going to a place full of magic and wonder called Civil Bend. Enjoy the ride.

PUTTING UP HAY

I was born on Valentine's Day, February 14, 1936, smack in the middle of the Great Depression. My mother and father were Fannie and Russell Bruner of Civil Bend, Missouri. I was the youngest of fifteen children: eleven boys and four girls.

I grew up on my Dad's forty-five acre farm. I went to school every day, save for summer, Monday through Friday, and Sunday school and church every Sunday, unless I was sick. That was orders from Dad, and he meant what he said.

When my chores were done I had the freedom to do whatever I liked, as long as I behaved myself and stayed out of trouble. I had complete freedom from about the age of five to explore every inch of ground within a radius of a mile or so from our house. By the time I was a young man, as a result of the way I was raised and given the freedom to rule myself, I had learned how to work hard, be friendly, play fairly, and behave myself at school, at church, and in public.

I have often asked myself why I was born in this isolated and completely safe world of hard working country folk. I was so happy. I felt safe and loved. In high school I was a star in sports. Everyone liked me and I them. It is almost mystical to have had the privilege and honor to grow up in this paradise, in this family, in Civil Bend.

I grew up as a toddler during the Great Depression, but I don't remember ever hearing the word poor, and I certainly never felt poor, even if we lived in a house without electricity until I was five and that never had indoor plumbing while I lived there. I also grew up during World War II and was aware that I had two older brothers fighting in a war against some very bad people, though I always felt, and was, safe.

One thing that did change over time in my years in Civil Bend was my relationship with money, and a few stories about that may help you to better understand my isolated paradise. When I was eight years old, and this is the truth, a penny was a lot of money to me, and even by the time I was twelve a quarter was a small fortune. In my early teens Dad would give me a quarter to spend on Saturday night in the town of Pattonsburg, and I was both happy and grateful, never needing or asking for more than that.

My horizon expanded when I started eighth grade and began going to school in Pattonsburg, five miles from Civil Bend. As a result, my isolated world became larger, with even more freedom to explore whatever intrigued me. In Pattonsburg I excelled in academics and sports, receiving many school honors in a town that revolved around its high school. My heart, however, always remained in Civil Bend, where my character was formed, where my confidence was built, and where I learned I could be whoever I chose to be.

As a child, a penny or a nickel was all I needed, but that basic belief was challenged one day when an older brother sent me a dollar through the mail. I immediately understood that meant one hundred candy bars, but Dad cleverly took the dollar and said five candy bars a week was more than enough, and there was money here for plenty. I was then given five cents weekly, with instructions to keep track of and account for that money until it was gone.

That, in a nutshell, is what my stories, ultimately, are all about: how to humbly and gracefully evolve as we encounter increasingly complex circumstances. After all, pennies and nickels, and even dollars, are not enough to meet life's needs, so how do we meet the unfolding challenges and opportunities life presents?

When I started high school, one of the things I discovered for the first time was that I would have to learn to somehow make money on my own. After all, Dad was paying for my food, clothing, housing, education, and other things I didn't even know about, so I didn't want him paying for my fun as well. By the time I was sixteen I needed a few dollars a week to take a date to the movies, have a couple of hamburgers and sodas, put gas in Dad's car, and otherwise spend time with friends in Pattonsburg. I was also starting to think about saving money for college.

The summer of 1951, when I was fifteen, was the beginning of my working for serious pay. My brother Gayle had just graduated from Pattonsburg High School and left the Home Place at the end of May, leaving Dad and me alone on the farm. That year, my sophomore year, my best friend Charlie Blankenship asked if I wanted to be on a three man crew putting up hay. I jumped at the chance, even though I knew it would be hard work, and Dad said he would let me do that on Saturdays every week.

Charlie and I started to work the first Saturday in June, and I made a whopping $10 each week, and that was a fortune. And you may not think much about hay, or the crucial importance of hay for farmers, but putting up hay was essential to the well-being of northern Missouri farms such as ours, so we were also doing something important for our community.

For all that summer I would get up each Saturday morning at five a.m., do some chores and milk the cows, and then a truck would pick me up at seven on the nose, as we were needed in the field by 7:30. It was hard work, but now I had my own spending money.

I was fifteen years old and rolling in dough.

My how much has changed since then, when it seemed like I owned the world after a hard day's work, knowing I had done something important for my community at the same time.

Putting up hay, or making sure hay was properly prepared and stored for winter, was crucial for the success of farms in northern Missouri, and it was a process that occurred every summer at least three times, depending on the weather.

There were basically four different types of hay we grew on our farm. We could count on a maximum of three crops of alfalfa and two crops of red clover a summer if the climate cooperated. Lespedeza was considered good hay but took longer to mature, and two cuttings a summer was all you could count on. Timothy hay was always a large crop, but you would only get one crop per summer.

What is hay anyway? Hay is food for farm animals. It was food for our cows and their offspring. It was also food for our mules. This was wintertime food. In the summertime the cows and their calves, as well as the mules, would enjoy eating the grass from our pastures. The cattle and the mules got along just fine together, roaming the pastures, searching for the best grass they could find.

Farmers never feed hay in the summertime unless there is a drought and the grass dries up and you have no choice. The cows must be fed year round if you want milk to drink and sell; likewise, you must fatten the cattle if you plan to butcher a steer or two for food or sell those that remain.

People in large towns and cities don't realize how tough the small farmers used to have it. It was, and for many still remains, a risky business. Farmers have to have good weather if they are going to have a good year. The old saying "make hay while the sun shines" is only a half truth. You make hay if the sun shines, but there has to be plenty of rain mixed in at the right times.

We normally named the milk cows. Our two mules were Pete and Jack. The cows were normally named by their color, such as "Whitey" or "Blackie" or "Old Red." We seldom named the young cattle because we would get attached to them and then either sell them or butcher them for food. That's just the way it was.

In a few generations past, before my time came along, planting various seeds such as wheat, barley, oats, red clover, and alfalfa was done by a process called sowing. You would put a sack full of seeds around your shoulder by a strap, reach in with your hand, then cast the seeds back and forth over the prepared soil, like a Johnny Appleseed. Later an improvement was made by attaching a metal pipe to the bottom of a sack that had a small opening at the end, and you would sling the pipe from side to side, casting the seeds farther and making the sowing faster by covering more area. The problem with these two methods was that you could not get the seed to land evenly, and so you would have areas with very little seed and others with too much. By the time I grew up, another invention was made called a planter: a contraption pulled by mules or horses with a large bin about eight feet wide that planted the seeds in rows. This was a much more efficient and precise way of planting, with the seeds dropping about two inches apart in nice rows.

Next, nature takes over. We wait for the sunshine and the rain to come in proper intervals, and we wait and watch to see how the plants grow. When they get to the right height they are cut. The cut plants are then left in the fields to dry for a couple of days, and here the farmer hopes for no rain. Then you take another farm implement called a rake, pulled by mules, horses, or a tractor, and rake the cuttings into rows. You then come along with the mules, horses, or tractor pulling a wagon with a hay rack, and then you pitch the hay onto the wagon with a pitchfork, stacking it onto the hay rack. So that is the sort of work we were doing.

You need two people pitching hay onto the wagon and one person stacking it with a pitchfork until the hayrack is stacked as high as possible. Then the wagon is pulled to the barn and the hay is put up.

There are a couple of ways of putting up hay. Instead of hauling the hayrack full of hay to the barn you could build a huge haystack right there in the field. This is a process of stacking hay in what looked to me as a kid like a huge loaf of bread. It was shaped like that. In the wintertime you could load the hayrack from this large stack of hay a couple of times a week, take it to the barnyard, throw it on the frozen ground, and feed the cattle enough for a good meal. By the way, building a good haystack out in the fields is an art. If the hay is not stacked just right it can collapse on the edges, fall somewhat, and then the wind could blow some of it away.

ME AND THREE BROTHERS ON TOP OF A HAYSTACK, CIRCA 1940

Later on as I got older a new farming implement came along called a baler. The first ones were pulled by mules or horses and the hay was made into bales. These bales were hauled by wagon to the barn and then stacked in the barn. They were rectangular in shape and weighed about sixty pounds, held together by binder wire. This was a much better way of putting up hay, eliminating the old way of stacking loose hay, pitching it into the hayloft, and having all that loose hay falling on you.

By the time I was in high school the tractor had come along and replaced the mules. I was sad because we sold our mules and they were really like pets, and since they were old and couldn't work hard anymore they probably ended up as dog food. It is also true, however, that putting up hay became much easier. The new balers were pulled by tractors that spit out bales so fast you could not believe it. These bales now were tied together with binder twine instead of binder wire. The twine was cheaper and easier to break apart when feeding hay to the cattle or mules. Before long the balers became less expensive, paving the way for round bales about the same size and weight. Today the bales are round but much bigger, weighing about two hundred pounds, and a new way of wrapping them in plastic was invented so they could be better stored outside by the sides of fields and not put in barns anymore.

Just so you know, used binder wire had many uses on the farm, from tying things together to repairing certain things, such as tying up a gate to a fence post. Many times my Dad would say, "Go to the barn and get me a couple of strands of binder wire." We always kept the old binder wire and used it for things that are too numerous to mention.

There were other types of food, besides hay, that were harvested on the farm for the cattle, horses, pigs, chickens, and sheep; we even raised a couple of kids, or small goats. Those other types of food included wheat, oats, soybeans, milo, and corn. All these crops had to be harvested but in different ways.

Oats and corn were used primarily for food for almost all our animals. Some of the oats would be taken to town, or Pattonsburg, Missouri, about five miles away, to be ground up into a feed mixture, which was then brought home in large bags or brought to our house in bulk and put in a large bin, where it was later mixed with separated milk as slop for the pigs.

The mules were fed whole oats for part of their food along with corn on the cob and hay. I used to feed the mules gnarly or half rotten apples that had fallen from the apple trees and not fit for human consumption. They would eat them right out of my hand. I really enjoyed that, and I think they did too. I had to be careful not to get my fingers chomped! Their teeth were pretty big and sharp, and they didn't think about hurting your fingers because they were excited to get some dessert I guess.

Of course, some corn was fed to the cattle and the mules, but it was used primarily for young pigs and sows. Sows are female adult pigs kept on the farm their entire life for producing piglets. We had one boar, the adult male that serviced all the sows. As a child it seemed to me that he was the only pig that had any fun. Chickens were the recipient of a lot of our corn too.

When oats were ripe they were cut with a binder, which was a farm implement that cut and bound the oats in bundles and dropped them on the ground. These bundles would be bound with binder twine. After the entire field was cut and bound, the younger children would go pick up these bundles and stack them into shocks, standing them upright, with about nine or ten bundles per shock, and with all the shocks topped with a single bundle. This was done so that rain would not soak into the bundles but run off into the ground, keeping the other shocks dry. This was also done with wheat the same way.

In those days there was a threshing day, and there was usually a person who owned a threshing machine. It was a big machine that would separate the oat straw from the seed. I remember as a kid enjoying watching this. I can't really describe very well what this machine looked like. It had big pulleys and a motor that made a lot of noise. There was a crew that came with the thresher, and they traveled from farm to farm setting up their machine. Normally they could do the farmer's crops in one day and then move on to the next farm.

The adults, such as my Dad, and some of my older brothers would go to the fields where we had shocked the oats or wheat, and, with a wagon and pitchforks in hand, load the wagon with the bundles. They would then drive to where the thresher was set up, drive alongside the machine, and with the pitchforks unload the oats or wheat onto a conveyer belt and then into a big grinding bin. The seeds would then come out and be poured into a wagon or truck, and the straw would be spit out onto the ground or into another wagon. The straw would be kept if the farmer wanted to use it for various things such as bedding for animals when giving birth to piglets or calves, keeping them warm from the cold ground. The grain would then be taken to wherever the farmer wanted to store the oats for winter.

Three or four farmers always helped each other out, and when one farmer's threshing was done they would all go to the next farm and help them. When I was probably ten or eleven years old my Dad put me in charge of the lemonade for a threshing team: a ten gallon milk can half full of homemade lemonade and half full of ice for the threshers to drink, right there by the threshing machine. There was plenty, and boy was that lemonade good! After all, since I was in charge of dispensing the lemonade, I made sure to get plenty myself.

One year when about that same age I rode a horse with a saddle out in the fields and provided cold water for anyone who wanted some. I don't know whose horse it was, but it wasn't ours. I think it may have belonged to Grover Henderson, a good friend of Dad's. I really enjoyed doing that too, but my butt got pretty darn sore before the day was over. I wasn't used to riding a horse, even with a saddle.

As a final side story about cutting hay, we also had an old fashioned horse driven hay mower. When I was sixteen or seventeen it was kept north of our house, by the dirt lane that came up from the gravel road that went by our house. That gravel road started about two miles west from highway 69 through Civil Bend past our house on toward the Other Place. The mower by now had been converted to a tractor mower. I had mowed some hay with it, parked it to the north of the house, and then put the tractor in the barn. I had also, however, left the heavy arm containing the sharp sickle blades down in the grass. After the chores and supper was over my Dad looked out the kitchen window, which faced the south, and he noticed the sickle blades down, so he told me to go put the arm up out of the grass because the dew would rust the blades. In lifting the heavy arm I had to put my hands on it, and when I did so the sharp sickle blades went "psssst" and slid down an inch or two. Fortunately I was not gripping the points on the arm or I would have sliced some fingers off! What a tragedy that would have been. Plus, that would have been the end of my basketball and softball days too.

DAD WORKING WITH HAY IN THE BARN, CIRCA 1960

FANNIE RECK AND HER CHILDREN

My mother, Fannie Reck, was born November 21, 1893. The following is what family history I have on her, most of which was obtained from Aunt Elsie (Fannie's sister) and the family Bible we had, and from Myrtle Bruner, my oldest sister.

John Reich, Fannie's grandfather, left Mühlhausen, Germany and arrived in New York in 1857, heading to Ontario, Canada, where he traded the furs from animals he trapped and tanned to sell, though tragically, not surviving one of Canada's harsh winters, he was found frozen to death around 1865. His son, however, was Joseph Reck, my mother's father, who died in Civil Bend on May 17, 1931 and is buried in the Civil Bend Methodist Church cemetery.

Fannie married Homer Russell Bruner, my father, on February 1, 1911. According to the marriage certificate, Russell Bruner's place of residence was listed as "Trenton, Grundy County, Missouri," and Fannie's place of residence was "Holt, Clay County, Missouri." Those two towns are a little over sixty miles apart. Were they dating long distance? Why would this be? No one seems to know. Maybe Fannie was living with a relative and Dad was working for someone as a farmer? Russell would have just turned twenty-one, and Fannie would have been just seventeen. We all have to read between the lines and draw our own conclusions I suppose.

MARRIAGE PHOTO OF FANNIE RECK AND
HOMER RUSSELL BRUNER, FEBRUARY 1911

Fannie and Russell had fifteen children together, and I'd like to introduce you to each of them.

My oldest sister, Myrtle Esther Bruner, was born September 9, 1911 in Civil Bend. Myrtle was educated in the Civil Bend area schools and graduated from Civil Bend High School in 1929. She had three children with her husband Stanley: Sharon, and twins Jerry and Joe. Myrtle died February 12, 2015 at 103 years of age in Overland Park, Kansas. Though she left home before I was born, she and Stanley kindly took me into their home my first year of college, and they always treated me honorably and kindly.

Vern Wilbur Bruner, my oldest brother, was born November 17, 1912 in Civil Bend. He was hearing impaired. He married Rose Mary Oblazny on July 12, 1941, and he died October 30, 1997, in Cameron, Missouri. Vern came home when I was six or seven years old with his new wife Rose. She, unlike Vern, was completely deaf, and also, unlike Vern, could not speak. Speaking for her, Vern told me she wanted to hold me. She was in a rocker, and Vern said she told him to tell me that holding me made her very happy.

Marvin Olen Bruner was born June 15, 1914 in Civil Bend. Olen graduated from high school in 1932, and while it is hard to find a lot of history about Olen, here is a little set of facts I found in some letters. First, when Olen graduated from high school, he went into the Civilian Conservation Corp (CCC), which was part of President Franklin Roosevelt's public works program during the Great Depression. He was paid $30.00 a month for his efforts, and $25.00 went to Dad. He then hopped railroad cars to get to Chicago.

The reason Olen went to Chicago was because of the Great Depression, and Homer, his younger brother, had written him a letter, telling him to come to Chicago because there were jobs. Vern had also gone to Chicago, since chances were better there for the hearing impaired. Olen met his future wife Louise Henry there in the spring of 1939, while working in a drug store as a fountain manager to pay for his classes at Aeronautical University. After finishing his coursework, Olen went to work for Pullman Aircraft, and he and Louise were married November 19, 1941. The Japanese attack on Pearl Harbor was just a few weeks later, on December 7, 1941. Then came World War II.

Olen spent most of his life as an insurance salesman for National Life and Accident Insurance Company and did well in that business. He and Louise had two children: Russell and Barbara, and then, after retiring in Springfield, Missouri, Olen left this world on January 20, 1987.

Georgia Minnie Bruner was born on August 20, 1915 in Civil Bend, where she married Earl Bridgman on July 11, 1936, after graduating from high school in 1934. They had two children: Bernice and Earl Eugene. Tragically, the elder Earl died October 9, 1953, when he lost control of his automobile, while Georgia died many years later, on April 22, 1997. She once told me about how my mother was an excellent seamstress who made dresses out of 100 pound flour and feed sacks with patterns of flowers on them. She said the girls at school were jealous because she and Myrtle had the prettiest dresses in school.

Homer Delbert Bruner was born January 5, 1917, in Civil Bend. After graduating high school in 1935, he married his beloved Dorothy Kurtz in 1941 and they had two children: Bonnie and Cheryl. Homer was the first of all the Bruner boys to go to Chicago after high school. He went there to attend Coyne Electrical School and become an electrician: a goal he achieved. Homer was the person who wired our home in 1941 when we first got electricity. He worked in a restaurant before joining the army in 1942, and he later became a restaurant owner in St. Joseph, Missouri. I worked at his diner for two summers to pay for two years of college. He was always very generous, and I am forever grateful. Homer died on August 8, 1983.

Lowell W. Bruner was born on August 4, 1918 in Civil Bend. He never married, for he was killed in action in World War II on January 17, 1945. The date of death was confirmed on a telegram I distinctly remember my father receiving, a copy of which is still in my possession, dated February 3, 1945. Lowell was killed in Belgium during the final stages of the Battle of the Bulge, and he is buried there. Graduating from high school in 1936, he followed Homer to Chicago, where he apparently worked on a farm for a while, and then in a restaurant with Homer, until he too joined the army in 1942.

Lowell was killed near the town of Beck, Belgium as the result of a large 88mm tree burst. His company was digging in snow covered ground when the tree burst happened. We learned this from a person who was a member of his platoon. Lowell was in the 75th division, 289th regiment, company G. The conditions were terrible for this particular group of soldiers, and many were killed in a very short period of time between December 1944 and January 1945. You, if free, are free because of men like my brother Lowell and the many untold others like him.

Carol Pauline Bruner was born August 8, 1920 in Civil Bend, and she graduated from high school in 1938. I remember her talking to me one day when I was helping her snap green beans. She talked about how proud she was of her children, and about how proud she was of me too, and how she knew for certain I was going to grow up to become a good citizen. She had a way about her that made me feel important. She married Clifford Guy Burton April 21, 1940, and their children were Loren Rex and Phyllis. She moved to Earlham, Iowa in the 1950s where her husband worked until retirement, and she worked in Des Moines several years for Meredith Publishing. Carol died on June 7, 2010.

RUSSELL AND FANNIE WITH VERN, LOWELL,
MYRTLE, GEORGIA, HOMER, AND OLEN, CIRCA 1919

Miles Courtland Bruner was born December 13, 1921 in Civil Bend. He graduated from Civil Bend High School in 1939, and he returned there after meritorious service in World War II. A member of the U.S. Air Force, his plane went down after being hit by flak, which caused the failure of three of four engines. As fate would have it, and according to Miles by some miracle, they landed safely just inside France, returning from one of their many bombing missions inside Germany. Miles later married Doris Kathleen Warford on August 15, 1950, and when he retired from farming went on to become a high school counselor. They had two children: Doris Kay and Miles Courtland Jr.

At a family reunion in 2004, I asked Miles about the memories he had of what it was like when he was at home as a child, and what it was like when he returned home after World War II, before he got married. Here is some of what he said.

"When I was a young boy, we kept two cows at the Other Place during the day because the grass in the pasture there was much better than the pasture at the Home Place. Sometimes we drove the cows home to milk in the late afternoon, left them there overnight, milked them the next morning, and then drove them back to the Other Place, repeating the process until winter."

"We had two mules: Pete and Jack. Pete was born from a mare we had named Dolly. Dad purchased Jack from Grandpa Johnson. Pete and Jack made a pretty good team because Pete was hyper and more out of control while Jack was laid back."

"We had a separator and separated our milk, which means the cream was separated out of the milk. We sold the cream and fed the milk to the smaller pigs. The milk was mixed into a slop by mixing the milk with ground grains, probably oats, which we poured into a trough. I remember taking the runts of litters and physically moving them to an area of the trough where it was not as crowded. That way they could get enough to eat until they were big enough and strong enough to fight for their own food."

"There was a period of time when soybeans were used as hay. Soybeans became a good cash crop during the years 1945-1950."

"Basketball and fast-pitch softball were my favorite sports. In high school I played center, and we were not very good. We played towns such as Altamont, Jameson, Pattonsburg, and Gallatin. After World War II, I played fast-pitch softball for the Pattonsburg town team with Johnny. He was a very good pitcher, and I played first base. We played several town teams around the area, and we were pretty good. Town teams were put together by different sponsors as far away as St. Joseph that would come and want to play against us because of our team's reputation. Pattonsburg lost a few games but not many."

I just so happen to have a picture of that team from the *Pattonsburg Call* dated September 9, 1948. The title of the article was "Daviess County Champs." The photo was taken in front of the bleachers behind home plate at the home field in Pattonsburg, and I am visible in the stands, second from the right, third row from the top. Miles and John are third and fifth from the left on the second row. I would have been twelve years old and – believe me when I tell you –I never missed any of those games if I could help it.

DAVIESS COUNTY CHAMPS, 1948

According to the 1940 census, Vern, 27 years old, Olen, 25 years old, Lowell 21 years old, and Miles, 18 years old, lived together in a boarding house in Chicago. Vern was a waiter in a restaurant, Olen was a soda fountain clerk in a drug store, Lowell was also a waiter in a restaurant, and Miles was unemployed. After a good, long life, my brother Miles died a much-respected man on August 3, 2008.

Joseph Dean Bruner (aka Joe Dean) was born on October 30, 1923 in Civil Bend, and he graduated from high school in 1941, going on to become a dentist in California. He graduated from dental school at Northwestern University in 1945, moving to California in 1948 and practiced dentistry until retirement in 2007. Joe Dean became a dentist because he saw our mother pacing the floor with a terrible toothache, and he wanted to help people suffering that way. He married Doris Belok, and they had one daughter, Jevaye. Joe Dean died November 18, 2010, physically far from his family and the roots of his childhood, though near in his family's hearts.

John Russell Bruner was born on March 2, 1926 in Civil Bend, and he graduated from high school in 1943. He married Charlene (Midge) Robertson, daughter of Mr. and Mrs. Carl Robertson of Pattonsburg, Missouri, on September 2, 1951, where our brother Wendell served as the best man. Charlene and John had three children: Terri, David Roger, and John Leslie. Divorced in the early 1980s, John later married Carol Ann McKay, and he was a large animal veterinarian practicing in Wisconsin for many years, having earlier graduated from the University of Missouri with the appropriate degrees.

I also asked Johnny to tell me some of his memories of growing up at home and what school was like for him.

"We always got up early and did chores. I milked cows and fed them. I fed Pete and Jack, our mules. I remember butchering animals, and when I got older I realized that Dad was really good at bleeding out the hogs."

John went on to become a veterinarian.

"I remember Miles and Carol breaking a path in the snow for me when walking to school."

"I remember Mom washing clothes, using homemade soap and a large iron pot to heat the water. She insisted on us taking music. I hated music. Our teacher was Mildred Smith. There was some animosity there. The Reno children were her pets. Dean Reno was a really good actor, though, and I really did have to give him credit for that."

"I sort of got into trouble when Pete Hangley, J.M. Riggs, and I had to stay after school for shooting paper wads. Our teacher, Blanche Woods, kept us quite a while after school. J.M. said he had to go home to do chores, and Pete said he did too. They got up to leave and just pushed me along as well. Well, Mrs. Woods came straight to our house. Dad and J.M's Dad were on the school board. She explained that we had all left without permission. I told Dad that I wanted to quit school, and he said, 'Alright we have plenty of brush to work on, like cleaning off some of the brush at the Other Place,' and so I told Dad I would go back to school."

"I remember Lowell rubbing my cold ears on the way to school in the wintertime."

"When we got sick, carbolic acid was dropped on the hot cook stove to fumigate the house. Food spoiled much of the time, probably because we had no refrigeration except the ice box. Dad used castor oil for everything. Skunk oil was used quite a bit too. Dad also made onion syrup with onions, sugar and water boiled on the cook stove, with hard candy and whiskey mixed in for colds to stop coughing. Vicks salve was rubbed on our chests, and a warm dry dish towel was placed over that. I always thought that really did work for colds in general."

"All the boys wore overalls. After basketball practice at school there was no place to clean up. The basketball court was dusty and dirty. The wind would blow dirt all over us and blow the basketball around like crazy. On the first day of school each year, before we could even play basketball, we would have to bring hoes from home to scrape off the weeds that had taken over during the summer."

"We had homework, and we studied by kerosene lamps. Gas mantle lamps were much brighter and better to read and study by."

"I remember one Christmas we drew names at school, and I drew J.M. Riggs's name. Mom bought two toy cars: one for J. M. and one for me. One was a towing car and one was a coupe. Mom knew I preferred the coupe, so I got the coupe. Christmas of course was a big thing when we were little. We knew Santa would bring us something. I remember a sad story about Roger. He wrote a letter to Santa and asked for five or six things and put it on the tree, but somehow it got overlooked and Santa didn't see it."

Marian Ruth Bruner was born September 27, 1927 in Civil Bend, and she graduated from high school in 1945. She married Gilbert L. Hutchinson from Pattonsburg at her childhood home, and they had two children: Linda and Gilbert Alan. Ruth and Gilbert were great collectors, amassing a treasure of sweetheart oil lamps, considered by many as the best collection in the United States, as well as all sorts of lamps used in farmhouses before electricity. The two of them also ran the *Pattonsburg Call*, which was the local newspaper for the area, which included Civil Bend, for many years. Gilbert ran a charming weekly editorial called "The Ink Pot." Ruth died December 30, 1996, not long after the Grand River once again flooded Pattonsburg.

Charles Wendell Bruner was born February 18, 1930 in Civil Bend, and he was the last Bruner to graduate from Civil Bend High School in 1947. He married Jeannie Cloutier, and they had five children together: Debbie, Douglas, Nathan, Margaret, and Andrew. Wendell was a great practical joker as a boy, and he went on to serve honorably for many years in the military. Wendell was a career serviceman who served seventeen of a planned twenty-year career when he tragically died from suicide on October 10, 1968, likely the result of Post-Traumatic Stress Syndrome. We will never know.

Roger Flint Bruner was born September 20, 1931 in Civil Bend, and he graduated from Pattonsburg High School in 1949. He was always the calmest of all the brothers, and I never saw him getting into fights at home. Roger was a good athlete in high school and in the armed services, where he played basketball and baseball. He married Brenda Joyce Vaughn on January 11, 1958, and they had four children: Angela (Angie), Stephen, David, and Duane. Roger, like his two younger brothers, went on to become a pharmacist in southern Missouri.

Merlin Gayle Bruner was born August 21, 1933 in Civil Bend, and he graduated from Pattonsburg High School in 1951. Gayle married Harriett Karr on August 17, 1957, and they had four children: Gayle Lynn, John, Diana, and Lisa. He too became a pharmacist, just like me and Roger.

During the family reunion of 2004, I asked Gayle to speak to me about his memories as a child growing up on the farm.

"I remember playing a lot of games in the front yard. Hide and Seek, Sheep In The High Pen, Cops and Robbers, Horseshoes, Softball, and Handy Over. We played basketball also out where the big apricot trees used to be. There was a pole out there with a backboard behind the big brooder house. I never knew why we called it a brooder house. It was a pretty good-sized building. I guess maybe before I could remember they used it to raise young chickens. I should ask one of my older siblings about that. We played softball work-up out there also."

"I remember that you and I used to hit rocks and walnuts into the openings of the barn with sticks or boards for singles, doubles, triples, and homeruns. I also remember laying on blankets at night, looking at the stars and occasionally seeing a falling star. That was fun to see. I would listen to the older brothers tell stories. On really hot nights we would even sleep out there all night. Once in a while it would rain, and we would have to pick up our blankets and pillows and run into the house. If it just sprinkled, then we would try and wait it out. We played a lot of croquet too."

Finally, I, Lee Roy Bruner, was born on February 14, 1936 in Civil Bend, and I graduated from Pattonsburg High School in 1953. In doing so, I ensured that every one of Fannie and Russell's children graduated from high school. I married Donna Lea Barnett on September 25, 1957, and we had two children: Michael Lane and Lori Ayn. Donna and I divorced in 1970, and I later married Vivian Mariette Carl on April 6, 1973, and we had one child together: Penny Eleeza Jessica.

My mother Fannie, who died the day I was born, insisted throughout her adult life that her greatest purpose was to produce life, and, as you can see, she produced fifteen children who all lived rich, varied, and full lives.

Of course, there were many times as a child I thought to myself, "I wish I had a Mom." As a child I was bitter at times because I didn't have that loving hug or hand on my shoulder when punishment was otherwise about to strike. I have learned, though, that we come into this life to accomplish many things in order to grow and become who we want to be, and this requires challenges.

When my Mom left this world she knew what she was doing. I can tell you that life without a Mom was not only tough for me but everyone else she left behind, but I became a stronger person than I would have been otherwise had she been there to "bail me out" from time to time. That said, I have been told by very special friends that I am very much like my Mom, and I realize what a great compliment that is.

I will have more to say about my mother in other stories, but suffice it to say that she and my father raised their children well.

RUSSELL BRUNER, MY FATHER

I don't have a lot of history on my Dad, Russell Bruner. I know he lived almost his entire life on our farm from his birth in 1890 to his death in 1977.

All of my brothers and sisters, save for Myrtle, were born in the same house Dad had lived in since he was five years old, though tragically the house at the Home Place burned to the ground in 1975, only sparing the barn and the cellar. Dad then moved to Pattonsburg for a year or two, and then he moved to the nursing home in Gallatin, Missouri, where he lived for only a short time before his death. As a father, he was a great organizer, an exceptional disciplinarian, and a virtuous teacher of the value of hard work.

HOMER RUSSELL BRUNER, CIRCA 1968

Goldie Duffy Frost, who married my father in 1952, was born December 13, 1889, and she died November 17, 1978. She was a kind and generous stepmother and companion for Dad for over twenty-five years. Goldie spent several years contending with arthritis, but Dad was always active and in pretty good health his entire life, at least as far as I know.

Here are some little stories that exemplify his character.

Dad and I lived alone for one year, from the summer of my sophomore year to the summer of my junior year of high school. I know he bent over backwards so that I could play basketball and other sports, so I could work with a crew to make spending money putting up hay on summer Saturdays, and so I could otherwise enjoy my time in high school. I know he had to do the evening and Saturday chores by himself so I could stay after school for practice and earn my own money on weekends. He let me have the car about anytime I asked, and I wanted it to drive to school once in a while and for dating.

When I was twelve years old, in 1948, I came home from school to discover that Dad's left forearm was in a cast. He had broken his arm that day. The article in the *Pattonsburg Call*, suggesting just how hard my father worked, read as follows:

> *Russell Bruner of Civil Bend community had the misfortune of fracturing his left arm above the wrist, at his home last Thursday.*
>
> *Mr. Bruner had been pouring gasoline from a large drum and was attempting to place the drum beside a tree. His arm was caught between the drum and the tree. The fracture was the result.*
>
> *Dr. J. Z. Parker, of Pattonsburg, Missouri, reduced the fracture.*

In addition to being a generous father and hard worker, he was also a man of great character. Here, in an attempt to capture that character, is the obituary for my father written by Joe Dean, which appeared in the *Pattonsburg Call*:

> *Very rarely is a man of truly great character recognized here on earth. We usually regard greatness as being powerful, wealthy, intellectual, pseudo-intellectual, pious or pseudo-pious.*
>
> *Are these God's criteria for greatness? I don't think so. Not long ago the spirit of a great man left this earth. Some of his credentials for greatness were:*
>
> *First, a real faith in God. Second, courage in the face of adversity so great only God and he know the great hardships endured. Third, inspiration and leadership for his children, to ensure theirs would be a moral and secure future. Fourth, great and determined effort to put more into the world than he took from it. Fifth, proving that in the Great Depression a large family could keep itself off welfare, no matter how se-*

vere the hardships were, showing by example that determination and concerted effort could pull a family through. Sixth, nearly everyone that graduated from Civil Bend School has this man's signature on their diploma. This great man thought it was important to have a major voice in selecting the teachers who were to teach his children. He was on the Civil Bend School Board for twenty years. Most board members considered this an unpaid and thankless task, but he recognized it for what it was: an opportunity to aid in the development of all the children in the community. Few besides his family knew how much effort he put into it.

Are these some of God's criteria for greatness of character? I think so. The spirit of this great man is the spirit of my father, Russell Bruner.

I am sure that the spirit of my mother, of 15 children, who preceded him in death during the birth of their 15th child, constantly reinforced him and gave him the inner strength he needed to develop the children, left without a mother during their formative years.

Yes, not long ago the spirit of this great man left this earth. The reception this spirit received in heaven must have been one of the greatest ever experienced there.

One of his sons, Joe Dean Bruner.

I think that sort of says it all, even though there's always a lot more I could say.

Here is but one example of my father's character and his profound and loving influence on my life, but to make the example clear I'll have to explain a bit about my role on the Pattonsburg High School basketball team.

During my junior year in high school, the year we went to the State tournament for the first time in our school history in any sport, our basketball team was really good. We had a very tall team for a small town like Pattonsburg. We played a double post offense because we had two players that were 6'6" and 6'5", so in effect we had two centers. We had one forward who rotated from side to side, one shooting guard who would play forward depending on the play that was called, and one guard who would call the plays. You might call him the quarterback, and that was the position I was fortunate enough to play.

It was my job to read the other teams' defense. Were they playing zone or man -to-man? Once I signaled what the next play was going to be, which was cleverly disguised, every player on our team knew their job. It might be setting a screen, or blocking some defensive player, or positioning for a rebound.

I was playing my position because I was pretty quick-witted, and the team had unanimously voted me their captain, with the approval of our coach, and so in many ways I felt especially responsible for our team and its success.
So here is the story.

Since Pattonsburg was only 40 miles south of the Iowa state line, a coach in a small Iowa town about 60 miles away had been following our team. He called our coach and asked if he might schedule a game with us. They could come to Pattonsburg. At the time, his team was 9-0 and ours was 10-0, and soon enough our two undefeated teams met to compete.

By the time the game was played, both teams were 11-0. We were excited to play the game, and everyone in the Pattonsburg area was also excited. The gym was packed, though the gym was always packed for all of our home games, but this was something extra special. My Dad, my brother Miles, and my sister Ruth were always there to support me and our team, and it was a very good game and close all the way.

With less than a minute to go we were down one point and they had the ball, stalling to run out the remaining time. Fortunately, they passed the ball to the player I was guarding and he mishandled the ball, so I quickly stole it from him, driving the length of the court and hitting a layup with only a few seconds left on the clock. The crowd went nuts, and victory was ours!

Yet, in the midst of all the celebration and excitement, I suddenly realized that the referee had blown his whistle, negating the play, saying I had fouled the player when stealing the ball! He was flat out wrong and I knew it. I didn't lay a finger on that player, and yet the basket did not count, and we lost the game by one point.

After I had showered and gone to the car, Dad was waiting for us to go home together. I was really upset, and Dad asked me what was wrong. I angrily told him, "I didn't foul that player! He mishandled the pass and I did not foul! The referee made a terrible and stupid mistake."

Before I could start the car Dad said to me, "You will turn your suit in tomorrow."

I said, "What?"

He said, "You heard me. You will turn in your suit tomorrow."

I said, shocked at his response, "I don't want to do that! I am an important part of our team!"

He paused for a while, thinking, and then he lectured me on the virtues of winning and losing.

My Dad said, "That isn't why you play sports! Everyone prefers winning over losing. You just learned a good lesson in life tonight, if you can grasp it. Life has its ups and its downs. Learn from the ups and learn from the downs. Whether the referee made an error is not what is important. What matters is how you respond and what you learn. If he did make a mistake, then I promise you it won't be the last he or anyone else ever makes, including you. I am sure you're disappointed, but it's just a game, and that referee, like all of us, is just trying to make the right decisions in difficult circumstances. I will let you stay on the team, but if you ever complain about a referee's call again you will be off the team. Do you understand what I just said?"

I said, "Okay." What else could I say?

I had a Dad who meant what he said.

I started the car and we drove home in silence.

That night I did not sleep well. All that was on my mind was losing the game and what Dad had said. Dad was a good teacher, showing me how to behave. Everyone makes mistakes in life. It's a difficult lesson to be sure, but overcoming what we call "unfair" is an opportunity to grow from the challenges that inevitably occur in life.

That season our team went on to lose three games, winning nineteen. Dad showed his love once again when, unannounced, he took a bus clear across Missouri, to the southeast corner of the state, to see me play in the State championship tournament in Cape Girardeau. He came to see me at halftime while the coach was talking to us. I could not believe he was standing there. He wanted me to know he was there for me, and I did not see him again until I got home from the tournament.

Not three minutes into the last half of that game a player on the opposite team and I were going after a loose ball. He landed on my already bad knee and tore it up again. The injury was so bad that one of my teammates had to carry me to the bench. My father, of course, was watching.

While sitting on the bench, watching us lose, I thought how disappointed Dad must have been, knowing I couldn't play in that important game, or perhaps ever again. Still not fully grasping the lesson he sought to teach me, I thought he had simply wasted a couple of days to come watch what happened. But no, that was not right at all. I now realize that it was just another "down" in his life that we happened to share, and he was a man who had many "downs" in his life, and we got through that one just fine, together. My high school career was not over, and during the following months I healed enough to play again my senior year.

Thank you, Dad, for being a wonderful man.

A PICTURE OF MY FAMILY IN 1935

Here is another nice picture of the sort of life Fannie and Russell created on our farm, taken directly from a newspaper article that appeared in the *St. Joseph Gazette*, dated December 22, 1935, just two months before I was born.

BRUNER FAMILY, CIRCA 1935

FOLKS MEET THE BRUNER FAMILY: SANTA CLAUS HAS BIG TASK WHEN HE VISITS FARM HOME

But Mr. and Mrs. Russell Bruner and fourteen children are awaiting him

MAKE THEIR LIVING ON 45 ACRE FARM

Higher education for each child is aim of father and mother

Special to the News Press—Pattonsburg Mo. Dec 22. Santa will find a real task awaiting next Tuesday night when he stops at the home of Mr. and Mrs. Russell Bruner and their fourteen children, six miles south of Pattonsburg. But he will come—the tree is already in place and he has never failed them.

"I always delay putting up the tree as long as I can," says the forty-two year old mother, who looks much younger than her years. "It always makes us so crowded."

The house is a large two-story framed building and the average size family would find it almost too large, but there are sixteen of the Bruners. The children are: Myrtle, twenty-four; Vern, twenty-three; Olen, twenty-one; Georgia, twenty; Homer, eighteen; Lowell, seventeen; Carol, fifteen; Miles, fourteen; Joseph Dean, twelve; John Russell, ten; Ruth, eight; Wendell, five; Roger, four, and Gayle, two.

PRAISE FROM TEACHERS

The Bruners' home is located on a forty-five acre farm. The proceeds from which has fed and clothed all the children and provided for their means and their grade school and high school educations. The Bruners plan to send all their children through the Civil Bend consolidated school, one mile from their home.

Seven of the children are attending school there this year. The number remains about the same, according to the Superintendent, James C. Lovejoy, because as one is graduated, another enters the first grade. The superintendent and all the school's teachers, Miss Elizabeth Hull, J.D. Breeden, Ralph Shaw and Miss Mildred Smith, have members of this family in their classes. This year the Bruners are represented in the senior, sophomore, freshman, 7th, 5th, 3rd and 1st grades.

Their teachers say these children are more socially inclined than the average child, they are very popular with their classmates and as agreeable as children can be. "I have two of my own," says Superintendent Lovejoy, "and they make more disturbance than all the Bruner children."

ONLY ONE BRUNETTE

All the children are above the average in intelligence and each seems to have his own particular talent. Lowell, the senior, is an outstanding athlete and has been called the best basketball player in Daviess County. He sings in the school quartet. Carol is the only brunette in the family, a condition which makes it impossible for her to wear the same colors as those worn by her sisters and therefore makes it necessary for her to have new clothes. Such an accomplishment by a member of this family is ample assurance of her ingenuity. Carol is particularly adept at drawing. John is outstanding in penmanship.

They are seldom absent from school. So far this year two days' absence has been marked up against all seven of them. They are always clean and attractively dressed.

The Bruners attend Sunday school at Civil Bend Methodist Church where they make up about one-third of the congregation. They are very much in demand for church and school programs and rehearsals are no problem at all when the participants all live under the same roof.

OBSERVE EVERY BIRTHDAY

Georgia helps with the cooking and housework. She considers Christmas the best time of all the year, although there are a lot of other "big" days. Every birthday is observed and they come in every month except April, May and July. August and September each have four in them.

Mr. and Mrs. Bruner believe that people who do not want large families do not know what they miss. They are proud of all their children. "We have no favorites," Mrs. Bruner claims, "although we have possibly humored Vern more than the others." Vern was born deaf. The defect wasn't discovered until he was about two years old. He was sent to the school for the deaf at Fulton, Mo. when he was fourteen years old and remained there for seven years. When he returned home he was equipped to fill his place as a useful citizen, an attainment which seems to be the ambition of every member of this remarkable family.

Lowell is planning on entering an electrical school in Chicago early in January. He expects to pay for his own way in college.

DAUGHTER IN COLLEGE

The oldest daughter was educated in Missouri Wesleyan College in Cameron and was later graduated from Central Business College in Kansas City. She paid for her college education by working while attending school and by obtaining jobs on nearby farms during vacation. Mrs. Bruner believes that if children are not interested enough in higher education to obtain it for themselves, there is nothing to gain by giving it to them.

MARRIED IN 1910

Mr. and Mrs. Bruner were married in 1910 [sic] when Mr. Bruner was twenty-one years old and Mrs. Bruner was seventeen. They began housekeeping on the farm where they now live and which they bought after they had been married about nine years. In recent years they have rented 135 additional acres.

All the children are at home now except Myrtle who is employed as a stenographer in Kansas City, and Vern who is in a hospital in Tarkio, Mo. receiving treatment for his eyes. They will be home for Christmas.

One job isn't enough for Myrtle, being a member of this family. She takes care of three little boys before and after office hours. Last summer she brought them to her parents' home on a visit. "They were used to quite different menus and didn't know what to make of our way," said Mrs. Bruner, "but before they went home they were enjoying our meals as much as my own children do."

MEAL TIME IS A BIG EVENT

Evidently Mrs. Bruner's meals are healthful as the children have never had any serious illness. Georgia gave the following as an estimate of the meals at the Bruner household: "For breakfast we have a half-gallon of gravy, about three dozen biscuits, half-gallon of stewed fruit, about a half-gallon of oatmeal, some meat, coffee and milk. A three-pound square of bacon lasts about two meals. We don't often have pancakes because it takes over an hour to fry them."

"Our noon meals require about five pounds of meat and more than a gallon of mashed potatoes. A large sack of flour lasts one week. One cake and three pies lasts one meal."

Mr. Bruner estimates his grocery bill at about $4.15 per week. A little over 59 cents per day. But, he adds, "We kill our own meat, raise a large garden, milk eight cows and have some fruit trees on our place."

EACH HAS OWN WORK

The Bruner home is popular with young people of all ages and every child in the community considers it an ideal place to come and play. Each child in the home has his own work to do. At present, Mr. Bruner and two of his boys are working on the graveling of the road which goes past their farm. When the community failed to get government aid to build the road, the Bruners and their neighbors decided to get "out of the mud" by their own efforts.

The Bruners are not on relief. The remarkable achievement they have accomplished with a forty-five acre farm is an indication of what can be done and furnishes a noble example for the millions of unemployed who complain of their inability to earn their own living.

These children are receiving valuable instructions on practical economy. A knowledge of which is sadly lacking in the world of today. They are learning to meet the challenge of a demanding world with an indomitable spirit that does not accept defeat.

GROWING OUR ANNUAL GARDEN

The garden we grew just outside of the house, about fifty feet or so just south of our cellar, was huge. It was a large L-shaped garden about the size of a football field going south, and the L-shape was on the south end going east. That part was probably fifty yards east-west and thirty yards north-south. Our well was down there at the middle edge of the east-west part. We had no running water in the house, and so we carried a three gallon bucket of water from the well to the house two to three times a day for drinking and cooking. The gravel road past our house was right next to the east side of the garden.

Just north of the well was our blackberry patch, which was about half the size of the north-south part of our garden going all the way to our front yard. That blackberry patch produced hundreds of gallons of blackberries every summer. We boys picked them every other day, and it was a nice cash crop for Dad, plus providing all the blackberry cobblers we could eat all summer, plus canning blackberry jam and jelly to put in the cellar for all winter. Those blackberries sold for fifty cents a quart or $1.75 a gallon. That was a lot of money back in the 1940s. That blackberry patch was also chigger heaven, but Dad had a recipe for preventing chigger bites. He dusted our arms, legs, waists, and just about our whole bodies with sulfur for almost a week. That really did work, and having yellow skin for a while was better than those chigger bites.

Just west of the blackberry patch was a row of grapes planted by my brother Homer right after World War II. They did quite well and kept us in grapes all summer, as well as lots of grape juice through the winter. Dad really liked grape juice, and every Sunday in the winter he would bring up a half gallon from the cellar that we drank after supper as a special treat. We would also sometimes have some for breakfast.

Just west of the grapes was a row of peach trees the same length north-south as the blackberry patch and the grape vines. Those were pretty good peaches, and we had plenty to eat all summer. We also canned some to put in the cellar for the winter. I loved peach cobbler and fresh sliced peaches with milk and cream, and a little bit of sugar wasn't bad. When we would peel peaches to eat we would take the seeds and throw them outside the fence rows, and a lot of volunteer peaches were all over the back yard and barn-lot fences. Some of those peaches were clings, and so my sisters would pickle them and can them, and they were a wintertime treat also.

My brother Johnny once told me a story I'd like to share concerning those peach trees west of the blackberry patch. On the north end of that row of peaches closest to the house was one tree that was different from the rest, and the peaches it produced were much bigger and better tasting. When he was four or five he was out by that peach tree and one of those nice peaches had just fallen off the tree. This was Dad's prized peach tree. I think he had planted it originally and it was his favorite. Johnny picked up the recently fallen peach, ate a ring around it, got full, and then threw the rest on the ground. Dad and Mom were there, and Dad came over and asked Johnny if he knew who had eaten some of that peach and thrown it away? Johnny said he did it, and he could tell Dad was pretty upset, and the ring around that peach probably didn't fit someone else's little mouth. Dad scolded Johnny, saying it was wasteful and not to do it again. He thought for sure he was going to get a spanking but someone came to his rescue! Who else but Mom. She brought him into her apron and Dad backed off. Now I never knew my Mom because she passed away when I was born, but Johnny told me she was a loving mother. I get choked up every time I hear stories like that about her. In fact, I'm getting choked up as I am writing this story right now.

The Bruner children grew up with a father teaching us right from wrong and how to make good choices, and with a mother's love, wanting to protect us from punishment or sorrow, when all that was necessary was learning a life lesson. We all grew up knowing the difference between right and wrong and making good choices with kindness accordingly. That feeling of guilt, when we knew we had made a decision that was not the right thing to do, was always there in our hearts.

We also grew a lot of apricots. We had four large apricot trees, the likes I have never seen since. I think Dad or Mom ordered them through a catalog. They were a hybrid of some kind, but those trees were thirty feet high at least and produced like you never would believe. They were growing west of our large garden. I remember going out there with my little red wagon, filling it with apricots and taking them to the house. That was another fruit that was canned and put in the cellar.

When I was getting ready for my senior year in high school, Dad remarried a wonderful lady: Goldie. She treated me like a prince, and she knew me pretty well. I would come home from college for a weekend when I could. I can still see her sitting in a chair in the living room talking to me and saying, "Guess what we are having for supper?" I would say, "Well, what are we having for supper?" And she would say, "Your favorite thing: apricot cobbler."

GOLDIE DUFFY FROST BRUNER, CIRCA 1968

Well, let's just say that raising things properly in the garden was very important. Remember, we grew our annual garden because we had to feed ourselves during the Great Depression and World War II, and it's not like today with the grocery stores in the cities. We grew sweet corn, potatoes, cabbage, peas, lettuce, carrots, onions, sweet potatoes, radishes, parsnips, cantaloupe, beets, tomatoes, turnips, cucumbers, watermelon, green beans, lima beans, asparagus, strawberries, popcorn, and even peanuts once. That's what we grew. Some vegetables I do not ever remember growing were spinach, broccoli, leeks, Brussel sprouts, or cauliflower.

Remember, our garden was about 300 feet in length. The garden ground was prepared the same way as the ground for planting crops in the fields. Our garden was an especially good plot of ground, meaning it was richly fertilized with manure from the barn stanchions where the mules were kept. That was a chore I certainly did not like. The manure would be about a foot thick and you removed it with pitchforks. This was done in the wintertime when working up a sweat was more difficult and the stench was not as bad, but it had to be done.

THE CELLAR

Let me tell you about our cellar, why every farm needed one, and what it looked like.

THE CELLAR AT THE HOME PLACE, CIRCA 1979

Our cellar was located about thirty to forty feet west of the house where I was born and raised, and it survived the fire that burned that house down. The cellar was on a slight rise in the land of maybe five to ten feet. When I was a young boy the door to the cellar was a regular upright wooden door that opened outward to the left, with a shelf inside just to the left and a solid wooden wall to the right. You then walked down about eight concrete steps that were about four feet wide, while the cellar itself was about eight feet wide and twelve feet long.

At the foot of the stairs was an overhang about five and a half feet high. As I got older I had to duck my head to walk in. We had electricity installed on the farm when I was five years old, and an electric outlet was installed overhead with a small ball-bearing chain to pull to turn on a light bulb that would light up the dark areas. There was a large wooden bin built on top of a concrete floor to the left, or on the south side of the cellar, and a wooden raised floor supported the bottom of this bin. The bin itself was about eight feet long, or the full length of the floor of the cellar, and this was where our harvested potatoes were put for the winter. The raised floor was for air to circulate around and through the potatoes to keep them dry.

The temperature in the cellar was about forty to fifty degrees Fahrenheit year round. Over this area was a cement curved roof. Above the cement was some form of wooden support, to support the dirt that was placed on top and over the back of the cellar. If you were on the outside looking at the cellar, then you would have seen a curved mound of dirt where you could plant some flowers if you liked, but normally we just grew grass there.

Describing the rest of the cellar, it looked like this. To the right of the potato bin was a two foot-wide path going the length of the cellar, and directly above this path was where the mound of dirt was, on the outside and up above. To the right of the path were four or five shelves that went from the floor to about five feet high. These shelves were about two feet deep, with about ten to twelve inches separating the shelves, which were also made of wood. These shelves were where the canned fruits and vegetables were put.

I remember getting into trouble one time when I went down in the cellar and opened up jar of canned mincemeat that tasted oh so good. I probably ate a couple of tablespoonsful and put the lid back on, and then a couple of days later I went down and ate some more. That went on for a couple of more times, until my Dad noticed it when he went down for some potatoes or something. He asked me about it and I got a spanking for that.

I haven't had a mincemeat pie since I was a kid. You cannot buy mincemeat in the grocery store and I doubt if anyone alive even knows how to make it. The meat in it was beef or venison. We didn't hunt deer so we always used beef. You can buy mince minus the meat, which contains a mixture of cloves, cinnamon, nutmeg, raisins, tomatoes, brown sugar, and apples. I have had pure mince pie, but without the meat is isn't nearly as good.

The other main use of the cellar besides for storing food was for shelter in case of a really bad wind storm or rain storm or the approach of a tornado. It was a perfectly safe place to go and wait out a storm. I remember going down there several times for safety growing up on the farm.

THE WALNUT GROVE AND MY PROTECTED WORLD

Behind our house to the west about twenty or thirty feet was a fence that went south, past the back of the cellar, all the way to the end of the garden where we kept our pigs. There was a small gate straight west from the back porch, and that fence line led into the walnut grove. The walnut grove contained at least twenty walnut trees and encompassed about two acres, with the trees populating the north half.

OUR HOME PLACE, CIRCA 1965, CELLAR LEFT OF HOUSE

In the fall, when the walnuts would fall from the trees, we would pick them up in buckets or bushel baskets and carry them to the lane, hulls on, and dump them there. Then the car tires would roll over them coming up and going down the lane. We would leave them there for a couple of weeks, then take the hulls off and put them on top of the brooder house in the middle of the south side of the grove. The reason we did this was because the area between the hull and the hard walnut was really black, slimy, and wet. If we worked otherwise, then our hands would get black from the walnut stains, almost impossible to wash off. By leaving the walnuts in the lane the hulls were mashed off and became dry, and then it was much easier to remove that outside layer without getting our hands too stained.

We would take these hulled walnuts, which would still be a little wet, and put them on top of the brooder house where the sun would shine on them, dry them, and cure them for cracking. Pieces of wood were nailed to the roof of the brooder house shingles to keep the walnuts from rolling off, and then we would spread them out one deep, and it looked sort of funny seeing that layer of walnuts on the roof drying out. After about two weeks drying out, we would take the walnuts down, put them in a container of some kind, and then crack them open with a hammer, one at a time, take the nuts out, put them in jars, and then use them for making cookies, cakes, fudge candy, or whatever called for walnuts.

This was all pretty tasty stuff, but harvesting the walnuts from our walnut grove was time consuming. Still, that was the kind of stuff that kept us out of trouble. It was also a sort of punishment when we got into trouble.

Another thing I did in the walnut grove was play make believe professional baseball. I would gather up about a bushel of green walnuts and set them on the ground about thirty feet from a tree, and then I'd pretend I was a pitcher for the St. Louis Cardinals baseball team. I would throw those walnuts at a tree, and if I hit the trunk of the tree, which was marked two feet above the ground and again five feet above the ground, then it was a strike. If I missed the tree altogether or below or above the marks it was a ball.

I started each inning with the bases empty. If I could strike out three batters before I walked four batters, then that was a scoreless inning. I would give the Cardinals three runs before the game started. If I allowed less than three runs in nine innings, or twenty-seven outs, then we won the game. If it ended in a tie, then I would have to pitch two scoreless innings after that in order to win the game. I would really get into it. I would say, "Harry the Cat Brecheen is winding up, here comes the pitch, STRIKE one. Here comes the next pitch, the fans in the stadium are tense, outside, BALL one!" One day Dad snuck up behind me. I thought he had gone working somewhere. He stepped on a stick or something, I turned around and he said, "Who is winning?" I guess I was a little embarrassed, and I'll bet he had a little laugh out of that. Later on in high school, when I was the starting second baseman for the fast pitch softball team for three years, all of that throwing practice made me an accurate thrower. I am sure of it.

There was another baseball game Gayle and I used to play in the walnut grove, and it went like this. There was a fence going from the back yard past the south side of the barn, about twenty to thirty feet away. We would stand on the south side of the fence with homemade bats made out of boards carved with handles on them, about three feet long, and hit rocks, walnuts, or what-ever we could find into openings on the south side of the barn.

THE BARN AT THE HOME PLACE, CIRCA 1975

Let me describe what the holes in the south side of the barn were, as there were several. Each one, while having its practical function, also counted for something different in our game. There was, first of all, a pretty large opening in the middle of the barn, which you can see in the picture above, where we would keep the wagon or milk the cows in the wintertime. When we eventual-ly got a tractor we kept it there. That opening was about twelve feet wide and eight or nine feet high. This was the singles opening. If you hit whatever you were hitting there, then you got one base.

If you could hit the roof of the barn and your projectile continued over the barn, then that was a double, or two bases. There was another opening on the far right side of the barn where the mules went in to be tied up for the night. That opening was about five feet wide and eight feet high. That was the triple opening, which counted as three bases.

Finally, about two feet to the left of the singles opening was the corn crib opening, where corn was shoveled from a wagon with a scoop, after the corn was picked and brought in from the fields. It was also used when we kids crawled up there to get a bushel or bucket of corn out to feed various animals, such as the pigs, chickens, mules, and cows. That opening was only about three feet wide and three feet high. That was the home run opening, which counted as four bases, which equaled a run.

When you were batting you would decide which opening you wanted to aim for, but if you missed the opening you were aiming for then you were out. If you aimed for the roof and you missed it, or if your walnut or rock did not go over the roof after you hit it, then you were out. It was a really good game and we had a lot of fun doing that. It also helped us later on in high school playing softball with our hitting. The only problem was that Dad would say to us, "You boys need to clean the rocks and walnuts out of the barn, and pick up all those rocks and walnuts in front of the barn too. I almost twisted my ankle out there today!"

I really did live in an isolated world. My class size in grades one through seven consisted of only four students, all boys. There were five students in my sixth grade class. The reason for that? A new teacher taught there that year, and she had a daughter my age. That was the only year in the seven years I went to school in Civil Bend that there was a girl in my grade.

I could have gone to school in Civil Bend my eighth grade, because that was the last year they had a school there. From that year on everyone in that school district would go to either Jameson or Pattonsburg. Dad let me go ahead and go to Pattonsburg that last year because Roger and Gayle were already going there to school.

I grew up on a farm and had a lot of freedom, living in a type of Eden. The reason I say that is because all my young life I roamed the farm at will, adventuring here and there whenever I wanted, as long as my chores were done. On a lot of those adventures I would see and hear things that I still remember about nature. I saw a mother quail up in the pasture at the Other Place, and trailing behind her were seven or eight baby quail. I just froze in my tracks, and they passed by me within ten or fifteen feet. I would see rabbits and squirrels, deer and foxes, and all kinds of birds. As a young child, I would get caught out in rains and skip rocks on ponds. I would find places to pick wild gooseberries and raspberries. I would find wild plum trees with the best tasting plums on them.

Dad would sometimes send me out to pick wild berries for making jelly. One time, when picking raspberries, I almost had a tragic encounter. I had just stepped over a ditch to reach some ripe berries and found myself straddling a dangerous rattlesnake, rattling ominously. It took a lot of standing still while it was rattling and rattling, until it slowly passed. I always wondered what would have happened if I had panicked and jumped back, for it certainly would have bit me. Another time, in the middle of a loaded gooseberry bush, when reaching in for a nice clump, I came upon a huge wasp nest, though I pulled away without any harm. Such were the limits of my natural dangers.

So there are lots of little stories that suggest how protected my world actually was. Sometimes, for example, I would walk down to the Other Place, where we often milked the cows. There was old farm machinery kept there, such as binders, combines, rakes, and mowers. I would go inside the house, which was no longer occupied, and go all through it, as if it were my own. It had a neat upstairs where I could look out the windows. One was the window where Wendell told me he saw Old One Eye.

On one of those days at the Other Place, Gene Bridgman, my nephew, four years younger than me, was upstairs looking around where an old ironing board was set up. Why I had no idea. On that ironing board was an old dried up cigar butt about two or three inches long, and so we decided we wanted to smoke it. We went to the Home Place, got some matches, and then brought them back. I being the oldest, probably twelve or thirteen, took charge, puffed, and lit it up. What a stupid and dangerous thing that was to do. I certainly had to know that was wrong for several reasons. Anyway, thankfully we didn't burn the house down, but we did get sick.

Believe me, I never did smoke cigar butts again.

Once in a while I would walk to Clinton Whetstone's house. He was a class-mate who lived a good mile away. There was always a chance he wouldn't be home, but if he wasn't then I would just come back. I walked there one time in winter, and there was always snow on the ground in winter as I remember, but I had overshoes on, with a stocking cap and gloves. Sure enough, this time he wasn't there, so I started back home and decided not to take the road, climbing over a fence and walking through some pastures, just to be different. While on this adventure I came upon a persimmon tree ripe with persimmons. I don't think I ever saw a persimmon tree in the wintertime with no leaves, just persimmons. They were practically frozen, but I tasted one, and it really tasted better than any I have ever tasted since. I bet I ate ten of those and filled my pockets. Persimmons, if they are not truly ripe, can be pretty bitter, but these were really sweet. I never did run across that situation again in my life.

Some people reading these stories might think, "What was Lee Roy thinking, wandering off like he did as a child, all by himself?" Well, my father must have known that I would be alright, and because of that faith I have always been willing to take a chance or do something a little risky, just for the sake of adventure. As long as it is not immoral or illegal, why not? Also, and this is honest truth as well, ever since I was twelve or so, I have always felt that I have angels or guides looking after me. I am not really afraid of anything anymore. I guess I could have been bitten by a spider or a snake and died in the woods, but those thoughts never did enter my mind. One of my favorite slogans or sayings is "go out of your mind and get into your heart."

One of the many reasons I really liked all the years I went to Pattonsburg High School was because of a deep friendship I formed with Charlie Blankenship. He was the only child in his family, while I was the youngest of fifteen siblings; he lived in town, while I lived on the farm. His life was very different than mine. He enjoyed that difference and so did I. We also had a lot in common. We played on the basketball and softball teams. He liked to come to the farm and get involved with my chores, even though he would make mistakes. He liked my Dad, and I liked his parents. Charlie was a good kid, and Dad liked him. His parents both really liked me. But there was one really glaring difference: he didn't have the freedom I had. I think his parents were really over-protective of him. He found it hard to believe I could wander off anywhere I wanted to. He had a bike but wasn't allowed to leave town. When I would stay with him, though, I liked staying in town. His Dad owned a restaurant, and they would feed me like a prince. I could have a cheeseburger or even two if I wanted. They pretty much insisted I have as many French Fries as I wanted with a soda or two, with pie and ice cream. He had a dog that was really nice that lived in their house. By golly, it was heaven.

Heaven aside, one could still make ignorant choices out of innocence. Given that I almost drowned as a young boy, for example, I realized it was important to learn how to swim, but when I look back and remember how I learned, I realize that my preferred training method was a little risky. When my brother Miles got out of the army after World War II, he purchased a farm next to our Home Place. He also built a small barn close to the Other Place, which he used primarily for milking cows. There was a small branch of the Grand River that ran by the barn, but often there was not much water in it, so he had to figure a way to get water to the barn whenever he needed some. So, to provide permanent water for his cattle, not only in a pond but in his barn, Miles rented a bulldozer and dug a pond. That was the precise spot where Wendell and I were working years earlier, when he caught Old One Eye looking right at us out the window of the house at the Other Place.

The pond initially had no water, but, right after Miles had bulldozed that big hole for the pond, he next dug a trench, putting in a pipe from the pond to the barn. He then filled up the trench and covered up the pipe with dirt. There was a natural decline downward from the pond to the barn, and Miles placed a big round metal container in the barn with a spigot he could turn on and off. By this mechanism, once the pond began to fill with water, so also would the container, and so the cows and calves could drink when penned up. That pipe went to the deepest part of the pond with another pipe running straight up, and when it rained enough, and the pond reached a certain depth, the water would cover that pipe, providing a never ending supply of water for his cattle.

I was down at that pond one day goofing around and noticed the top of that pipe and I got an idea, even though I couldn't swim. I was sure I could push myself from the bank to that pole. I would have to splash my arms and legs a little bit and grab that pole without sinking. Then I could push myself off that pipe and swim back to the bank. It was only about fifteen feet or so away. So I took my clothes off and tried it. It was a little more difficult than I thought it would be, but I made it. Now all I had to do was crouch on the pole, push off, and swim back to the bank. I'll admit I was a little afraid, but I knew I could do it. I pushed off, but I couldn't get a very good jump and it was more difficult getting back. Still, I felt good because I had swam a little bit.

I decided to keep practicing and tried it again. I got to the pole and it was a little easier. Great! I crouched on the pole, getting ready to push off, then pushed, but the pipe went backwards into the pond. I didn't know that the pipe wasn't strong enough to hold my weight, and then I started sinking. I had to get back to the bank, and so I just started moving my arms and legs and by golly I made it. I knew I had learned how to swim, even if it wasn't very far.

Now that I didn't have a pole to swim to I just swam out about eight to ten feet and turned around and swam back. I did that for about thirty minutes, going farther and farther. I started out not going out in the middle of the pond but just along the bank. Then I could go out farther in the pond. That was how I learned to swim.

This was probably not the smartest thing to do, since I was by myself, but I nevertheless felt proud. I told Miles at the table when we were eating supper that I had bent his pipe in the pond. He really got mad at me, not, however, for bending the pipe, but for learning to swim all by myself.

I also want to tell you about my first paid meal away from home, since it also suggests how isolated and protected my world was. It is hard for me to remember exactly how old I was when such and such happened, but the following events occurred when I was probably nine years old. Dad asked if I wanted to join him on a trip to St. Joseph, Missouri. He was driving there to visit with Homer, who at that time owned a filling station, or what we would call a gasoline station today, and he and his wife Dorothy lived in an apartment above. When you filled up with gasoline you could go inside, below their apartment, and buy a hamburger and a coke if you were so inclined. Homer purchased that business after World War II. We were also going to visit my sister Carol, who also lived in St Joseph with her husband Clifford Burton. Of course, I told Dad that I would really like to go with him.

We took off in our car, probably a late 1930s or early 1940s model. I have no idea what kind of car it was. I think I have been told by my older brothers that Dad liked Chevys and Pontiacs. I have never been able to tell even to this day what kind of car is passing me on the road or parked right next to mine. I do know that Dad didn't drive very fast, certainly not over fifty miles per hour, and probably closer to forty. "St. Joe" was about fifty miles away, and it seemed to take a long time to get there. We went through a small town or two, and all the highways were only two lanes wide.

Dad was not in the habit of passing cars unless they were going very slow and he could see quite a way down the road. We must have left around 11:00 am, and we had driven about an hour when Dad stopped at a filling station and told me to get out and come inside with him. I thought he was going to get some gas, but he didn't pull up to the pumps. When we got inside, the operator of the station obviously knew Dad, saying, "Hello, Russell!" This station was about ten miles from St. Joe and obviously a place Dad stopped to visit from time to time. Dad told me to climb up on a stool and told the gentleman I was hungry, asking me what I wanted to eat. I had absolutely no idea, so he ordered me a ham sandwich, saying "make it two." Dad asked me what I wanted to drink and I said, "Does he have Whistle Pop?" He said he didn't, but he had Nehi Orange, and I said that would be fine. We ate at the counter, and I sat on a stool with a red leather top that spun around. I thought that was really neat. I thought to myself, this is really something, eating a meal away from home. I had eaten at Grandma Johnson's house when I stayed overnight with her, but I'd never eaten at a place as neat as this!

GAMES WE PLAYED

We had all the necessities of life on our farm. We had clothes to wear. They may not have been new clothes, but we were warm in the wintertime and had gloves to wear, though it's true we wore hand-me-down clothing until they were pretty much worn out. We had plenty to eat with our large garden and fruit trees, and we raised our own beef and pork, so we never went hungry. Most of us kids had a quarter to spend on Saturday nights to go to movies in Pattonsburg that cost fifteen cents, and we were pretty satisfied with that, at least I was. Maybe the older kids were not as fortunate, I really don't know.

When it came to entertainment at home we played a lot of games when it was playtime, after our work was done. We had to look for forms of entertainment that Dad could afford. Playing softball was one of those games, and we usually had enough players to play work-up. This was possible because we always had a bat and a ball. I don't remember having more than two gloves, even if they were tattered and torn. Whoever played first base would get a glove and the catcher would get the other one.

In the game work-up you would have two batters, a pitcher, a first baseman, a catcher, and everyone else played infield or outfield somewhere. You really needed at least seven players to make the game interesting. The two batters had to keep scoring to keep batting and running the bases. If a batter got out by popping out to an infielder, or grounding out by being thrown out at first, or flying out to an outfielder, then he would have to go to the outfield and everybody else would work-up. The pitcher would be the new batter, the first baseman would be the new pitcher, and so on. If the first batter got on first or second and the second batter was not able to knock him in, or if the first batter was out at home, then he would have to go to the outfield and work his way back up to be a batter again. This process kept going on over and over so everybody played every position over and over until dark and we would come in. We played this game a lot in the summertime. We played all our games after supper and on Sundays unless something else was going on. Dad occasionally played with us too but not very often.

Kids who lived nearby would sometimes come by and join in on our games. There were farmhouses about every quarter to half mile, and the kids would walk to our house knowing that a game was probably going on and they were always welcome. This happened more on Sundays than weeknights. When the weather was nice, we would play work-up in the spring and fall when school was in session. Other kids at school would sometimes ask if there was a game going on after supper.

Saturday nights were reserved for going to Pattonsburg to the movies. This was another form of entertainment besides playing games. There was always a big crowd in Pattonsburg on Saturday night. The theatre always had a serial which came on before the actual movie and after a newsreel and a cartoon, like Bugs Bunny, Roadrunner, or Donald Duck. The newsreels were one of our few ways of learning about U.S. and international affairs beyond our protected world, usually consisting of about ten minutes of dramatic film clips from events around the world, but the most exciting thing was always the serial: a continuous story that always had a suspenseful ending that of course would be continued next Saturday night. It might be about the life of Superman, Lash Larue, or some other hero. The Saturday night movie was normally a western with singing cowboys such as Roy Rogers or Gene Autry. Popcorn at the theatre was a nickel. That would leave me with a nickel to buy something else when I would run around Main Street with a friend that I found before or after the movie to spend time with.

In a Sundry store across the street from the Binney Theatre they had a fountain drink called a "Chocolate Phosphate," and I could buy this with my remaining nickel. I really liked that drink, which I think was chocolate milk with some vanilla and carbonation. I would go there if my friend also had a nickel, and we would get one of those delicious drinks before we had to go home.

The movie was generally over around 9:00 p.m. and we didn't have to be back to the car to go home until 10:00, so that gave me an hour to walk about Main Street. I might run into other friends and visit. If I would run into my brothers they would ask me if I had spent my nickel yet. When older, my buddy Charlie Blankenship and I would go to the pool hall and play pool. We could play a game of pool for a nickel and we did not have to pay if we won, and sometimes we could play until time to go home and never lose. If I still had a nickel unspent, then I could save it for the next Saturday. I really liked Saturday night a lot. What a social event that was.

Like I said, Charlie's dad owned a diner on Main Street, and he liked me a lot. Charlie took advantage of that and would often suggest we go in there and ask his Dad if we could have a Coke, and more often than not he would say yes. Another nickel saved because then I would skip my chocolate phosphate. There was more than one occasion when his Dad, in a good mood, would even fix us a hamburger and some French Fries. Jackpot! I really did feel kind of guilty, hoping he would do that again. I was always friendly and thanked him, and I wasn't buttering him up because I really was thankful and he could sense that, I think. Remember, eating out was a special privilege for me as a teenager. I also didn't realize it then, but he knew I was a good kid and was probably glad Charlie and I were good friends. It didn't hurt either that his mother liked me a lot too.

Getting back to that pool hall, my brothers Roger and Gayle said they didn't go in there hardly ever because of all the cigarette smoke. It looked a little too tough for them. But Charlie, living in town, and his Dad, owning the diner right across the street, knew all those older men in there, and they enjoyed having us young'uns around. Even the owners seemed to enjoy us being in there. We were in the eighth grade then and both on the junior high basketball team, and they knew we would probably be on the high school team in a couple of years. Also, Pattonsburg was a basketball town, and folks in town knew my brother Roger was on the high school team and a pretty good player. Besides that, Charlie and I would take on any two of the older players in a pool match, they knew we were pretty good, and we would beat them more often than not.

When I was in high school I played primarily on the junior varsity basketball team as a freshman. I did dress out for the varsity team but seldom played. On the fast-pitch softball team I sometimes played on the varsity team as a pinch-hitter my freshman year as well. I batted left-handed, was very fast, and could bunt with the best of them. I was also pretty small and knew the strike zone, so I drew a few walks and was able to get on base to start an inning if the line-up was right. In my sophomore year I started on the varsity softball team in centerfield and as an occasional second baseman. That same year I was one of the top two substitute players on the varsity basketball team.

I started every varsity fast-pitch softball game and varsity basketball game when I was a junior. I was co-captain of both of those teams. I was on the only varsity basketball team in the history of Pattonsburg basketball to go the State tournament. It was considered possibly the best team in the history of that town, at least up to that point. That was in the 1951-52 season. We also had an undefeated fast-pitch softball team that same year. At that time there were no play-offs that went to a State tournament in that sport. I played second base every game.

The Bruner boys were all pretty athletic and intelligent. We picked up the rules and strategies of all sports and games very quickly. My brother Lowell, I was told, was the best basketball player of all of the Bruner boys. I remember seeing him only once in my life when he was home on a furlough in the summer of 1944. He was killed the next January. I was nine that February, and he was gone from home before I was old enough to remember him. I don't remember any of my older brothers playing any sports in high school except Wendell in one game and Roger, four years ahead of me, who was an excellent shooting guard.

My senior year our team lost our two tall guys and our shooting guard. We were not quite as good, but we did win our annual Pattonsburg tournament for the first time in seventeen years. Our softball team went 12-3 and went on to win our conference, but we weren't as good as the previous year.

So, as you can see, as a family we played a lot of basketball when we were young and in high school. We would go down to the Civil Bend high school outdoor basketball court and play down there when school was out, and we had a basketball goal set up at home where we played softball out in the pasture, next to our apricot trees. Later on, when I was in high school, we put up a basketball goal on the barn and shot thousands of shots practicing there.

Another game we played a lot of as a family was croquet. I would guess that only one person out of a hundred knows how to play croquet and the rules of the game. For example, how many arches do you need to prepare the court for a game? What does it mean to tight a ball? What does it mean to croquet a ball? How many strokes do you have left after you croquet a ball? How many strokes do you have left after you tight a ball? How many people does it take to play a game? What does it mean to be dead on a player? I could go on and on. If you can answer just those few questions, then you are one of those one out of a hundred people. There are many more rules and regulations besides those.

My Dad really liked to play croquet, so we always had a croquet set. The croquet set itself probably cost $15.00 in the 1940s. A set included six matching mallets and balls, plus a set of wire arches. Real expensive sets had iron arches. We never did have a set like that. The set also included two stakes and, of course, the rack all this equipment went in. Our set was never in real good shape, given how much it was used. The mallets and balls were made out of wood, the mallets would get chipped over time from mishits, the varnished mallets and rack would get discolored over time, and the painted stripes on the balls and mallets and stakes would fade.

You could play croquet with two players, which was most common, and just play against each other like golf or tennis. Three could also play against each other, but I always thought it was a better game with just the two players. You also could play with four players and play doubles, or partners, which I always thought was the best game of all. Yes, you could even play with six players, with two teams of three or three teams of two, but that could get pretty confusing.

I won't go into all the rules and regulations of the game, but, if you want to play, then buy a set and the rules will be included. There is a lot to remember when playing, and there is a lot of strategy. There is generally a lot of arguing during the game because you need to keep track of a lot of information. Partners of each team can talk to each other as much as they want. A lot of secretive whispering goes on during the game. It really is a lot of fun and takes about an hour or more to complete a game.

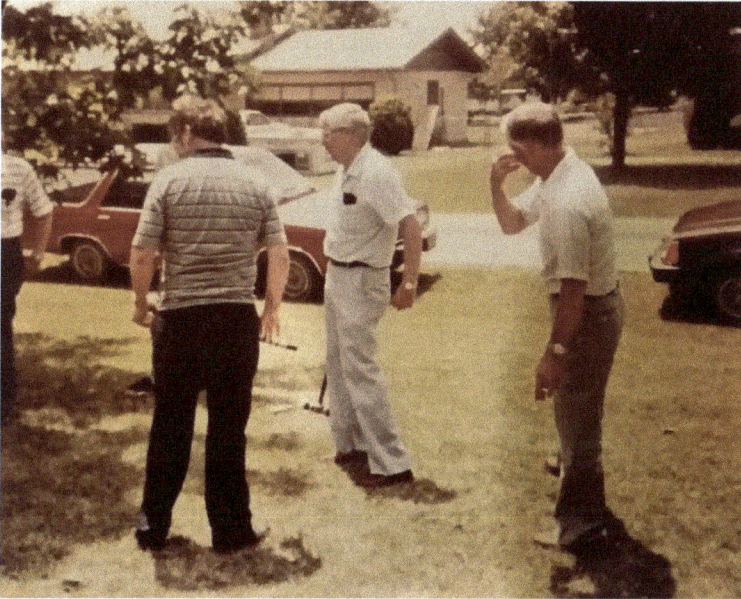

BRUNER BROTHERS PLAYING CROQUET

We generally played this game in our front yard, and sometimes quite a large group of spectators might appear to look or cheer on one team or the other. I started playing croquet when I was probably seven or eight, and that was probably when a lot of the chipping of the mallets occurred. Most of us guys got pretty good at the game, and the women played sometimes too.

The court can be made out of smooth dirt, and there was a court like that prepared by the men of the area just for them to play on, generally on Sundays. I do not remember that court, but it was apparently quite a place for men to go to on Sundays for a big game. That court, most active I'm told in the early 1930s, was not too far from our Home Place, maybe a ten minute walking distance. My father was one of the better players that would be there every Sunday afternoon to play. Some of my older brothers would be there watching.

My brother Johnny remembers an incident that occurred there when he was probably around eight years old that is too funny not to mention. Back in those days very few male children or adults wore underwear, as hard as that is to believe, but I can personally attest that I did not wear underwear until I was probably ten years old or so. My Dad wore long handled underwear in the wintertime and short handled underwear in the summertime to get by that dilemma. You must remember that people in that era in northwest Missouri farming country were not very wealthy, and buying underwear was not one of those items of high priority.

Johnny said this court was of exceptional quality and very smooth and flat, and the players were good and focused on each and every shot. Close to this court was a spring that fed a pretty good sized pond, and good fresh drinking water was available to the players if they wanted a drink. One of my other brothers, Johnny thought it was Lowell, got a big crawdad from the pond. While one of the players, Walter Canfield, was bent over sizing up his next shot and concentrating very deeply in a crouched position, with his torn pants and a certain body part partially exposed, Lowell snuck up and placed that crawdad in his pants, which then dutifully clamped onto that exposed part. When the pinchers clamped on, Walter, who was really concentrating, yelled from the pain and really got angry. It really was a laughing matter to everyone except Walter. Even though there were no women at this Sunday afternoon event, I am sure Dad was not too pleased to see this happen to one of his friends. This action by Lowell, though, typifies what I have often heard about him: that he was a very happy and mischievous lad. I am sure he was well-liked by the young ladies of the community, and the fact that he was tall and very good looking didn't hurt either.

Ping pong was another game that we played quite a bit. As a kid in school at Civil Bend in the fifth, sixth, and seventh grades we played ping pong a lot. There were three tables and plenty of paddles and balls, and we got pretty good at the game. Those tables were on the first floor of the school where the big furnace was, and it was always warm in the wintertime. We played ping pong at home, using our big dining table, which could seat ten, which made for a fairly good ping pong table. Over the years the dining table developed a warp on the tabletop, we would aim at that warp and it would deaden the ball with no bounce, and that would almost always win the point. We had a net that worked on that table, and even though the paddles were really worn out we still used them. Some of them were rubber sided and some were sandpaper sided. We would make them work. Ping pong balls were cheap, and Dad would buy a dozen every now and then. They would crack or get stepped on accidently. We would hit them too hard and cause them to crack and become useless.

We would play ping pong at night after we got electricity. Ping pong was really a year round game because we could play it at home in the summer too. We got a new ping pong set one year from one of my older brothers or sisters, and that was really nice.

Marbles was another game we played at school on the floor around the furnace, and we played marbles outside in the warmer weather at home, so marbles was another year round game we played. One time, when I was in the fifth grade, I sat down at my desk seat and my marbles fell out on the floor, and Mr. Bunting, our teacher, confiscated them and kept them on his desk, along with my special shooter. About a week later he told me to stay after school, and I thought I was in trouble for something. When everyone had left he asked me if I would like to play marbles with him for keeps. I said I would, even though I might lose more marbles to him. He played a game he had made up by having us try to throw them into a hole in the ground next to the foundation outside. It was a game he let me win. I got my marbles back, along with my good shooter. He told me to keep my marbles in my desk in a little jar and not in my pockets. They never did fall out of my pockets again.

We played hopscotch at home outside around the house. We would throw old used rubber jar rings to toss in the hopscotch squares. We played checkers and Chinese checkers. We had a carrom board and we played carrom. I never did know where that carrom board came from. I think it had been around for a long time. We also played hide and seek, cops and robbers, and cowboys and Indians. We used sticks for guns. When we got a little older we played a game called sheep in the high pen, and another called handy over, where you threw a ball back and forth over the roof of the house.

Handy over was a really fun game. You start with two players on either side of the house, invisible to one another, and one begins as the throwing team and the other as the receiving team. When the throwing side threw the ball, which in our case was a tennis ball, we of course couldn't see who on the receiving team caught it. One of them would only shout out, "We have the ball!" Now the goal is for the side now without the ball to get to the other side of the house without being hit with the ball by the receiving team. Or, conversely, the goal is to hit the team with the ball as they come around the house. So, how does one choose how to come around the house? The receiving team quickly has to make a plan. Who will carry the ball? Will they split up or move as a team? The throwing side will have to decide which side to come around as a team, hoping to avoid the person with the ball. If they choose correctly, getting to the other side without being hit by the ball, or if they get caught but the ball misses them, then they win a point. If they choose incorrectly and get hit by the ball they just tossed over the house, then they lose a point. If you hit one of them, then you won a point and got to throw over the house the next time. If you guessed wrong, then they would get a point and get to throw again.

When I got into high school I played a lot of tennis. I don't remember any of my brothers playing tennis, but things were different when Gayle left home to work with Homer in his restaurant and then go on to the army. I was the only one at home with Dad, I had access to the car a lot, and I could drive to Bethany where they had tennis courts. My buddy Charlie and I would drive up there about every Sunday and play tennis. Dad let me work for another farmer on Saturdays and I would make $10 a day, so I had more money to spend, and I bought a tennis racket and some tennis balls, would practice by myself by bouncing balls off the barn, and got pretty good at tennis. I even took a tennis class for my P.E. credits in junior college in Kansas City my first year of college.

Let's not kid ourselves. The most popular game at home was playing cards! As kids we played Old Maid. It didn't take very long, however, before we graduated to Pitch and a little later Pinochle. Pitch was an easier game to learn. There was seven point Pitch, ten point Pitch, and another version that I think we invented: thirteen point Pitch. We played those games as long as there were kids and grown-ups to play.

I was playing Pitch when I was only five years old. When they would play Pinochle I would sit by somebody and watch them play and bid. By the time I was seven or eight I was invited to play because they eventually needed a fourth person to make a game. They played single deck Pinochle and double deck Pinochle, but everyone preferred double deck. I remember my little hands could barely hold the cards in my hands, there were so many of them. By the time I was nine or ten I could play as well as anybody. At least I thought so.

Earl and Stanley, two of my brothers-in-law, were avid Pitch players, and we would play whenever they were around. They were fierce competitors. We played cards on many a Sunday afternoon after church and often well into the night, any night if possible. We played cards when it rained in the summertime. That was a good enough excuse not to work. When the wintertime weather was really cold or the ground was snow covered, that was also a good excuse to play cards.

We played a lot of board games such as Monopoly, Parcheesi, and others, but cards still dominated our free time. Other card games we played were Hearts, Spades, Gin Rummy, Solitaire, and Touring. A couple of games my brothers brought home from World War II were Clubs and Razzle Tazzle. Clubs was a three handed game that came in handy when only three players were available. Razzle Tazzle was a five handed game which came in handy when there were five persons who wanted to play. Another card game we played quite a bit of was Cribbage. We rarely played poker.

Obviously, we had lots of fun on the farm. Even though we worked hard, we also played lots of fun games that brought us together as a family and community.

HUNTING AND FISHING

Besides growing our annual garden and raising farm animals, another way we worked to feed the family was by hunting and fishing. When we got older, for example, we would go hunting for rabbits to eat. We always had a rifle or two and shotguns of various types such as a 12 gauge and a 16 gauge, all single shot. We had a double barreled shotgun on top of that. Johnny and Wendell were probably the best hunters that I can remember. Roger, Gayle and I were not big hunters, but by then we didn't rely on hunting that much for food. Stanley, Myrtle's husband, and Earl, Georgia's husband, were big hunters, and they used to come to the farm and hunt rabbits, bringing home a dozen or two to dress and eat. That was probably when I was about ten years old. Johnny and Wendell would go with them.

That leads me to a hunting story involving Johnny, after he had grown up and was probably a senior in high school, which would have been when I was about eight years old. He was at school with his friends, and one of those friends, Pete, said, "John, you know what we ought to do? I saw some ducks down at the river, you know, on the Donner Place. We should go down there after school and shoot some." Johnny thought about it, and thought it was a good idea, except it was March and duck hunting season was some time away. Johnny's friend said, "Oh so what, nobody will know the difference!"

So a bunch of Pete's buddies, including Pete's brother, Jack, J.M. and another fellow whose last name was James, and whose Dad was the Superintendent, all decided to get their guns and go down there. They met at an agreed upon spot. They all had shotguns except the James boy, and he brought his pistol. He obviously didn't know anything about duck hunting but just wanted to be part of the action. They drove down to the river together and parked their car.

They noticed a short distance away was another car parked in the area, and Johnny, knowing they shouldn't be hunting out of season and feeling guilty, said to his friends, "Oh my God, I bet that is a game warden checking the river area to make sure no one is hunting out of season!" J.M said, "Don't be silly. That probably belongs to someone who is fishing somewhere close by." So off they went and sure enough they had pretty good luck and shot a few ducks, while the James boy shot away with his pistol.

They were walking back to their car, it was getting dark, and they needed to get to their respective homes, when they noticed another car pull up a quarter mile or so from them and turn off their lights. Johnny's guilt came back into play and he said, "Darn it, I bet that's the game warden! What are we going to do? We have these ducks and if we get caught we will be in trouble!" They decided that J.M. should go to the car and drive to where they were, and they would just wait for him. They could just drive past the game warden with the ducks and their guns in the car, out of sight.

So before too long here came J.M. and they started home.

About that time the other car's lights came on and Johnny said, "Let's throw the ducks out the window in the ditch. It's not worth getting caught!" That is what they did, and they drove past the parked car with the turned on lights, and sure enough it wasn't the game warden. It was probably a couple just parked there, probably smooching, but the hunters drove home without their ducks. They were going to let Johnny have the ducks because Myrtle, our sister, was home while Stanley, her husband, was in the army. She would cook them and, knowing how many there were to feed at our house, would also know it was the right thing to do. Johnny went in and went straight to bed when J.M. dropped him off.

The next morning Myrtle asked Johnny, "Did you not have any luck last night? Did you not catch any ducks?" He didn't want to lie about it so he told Myrtle what had happened. She was upset and told Johnny, "You go back there and get those ducks!! As cold as it was last night those ducks will be just fine, and I will cook them for supper tonight." Johnny and another brother took Dad's car and got them and brought them home, and Johnny said they tasted mighty good.

Just a few years later it was on a nice summer Wednesday when I saw the mailman drive by, leaving something in the mailbox. Little did I realize that a big fishing expedition was in store. I was always excited for the mail to come, hoping one of my brothers and sisters would write me a letter. That seldom happened, but a letter to Dad would come once in a while saying one of them was coming home for a weekend or maybe even a week on their vacation, or one of my brothers in the war would write a letter. Also, once a year the mailman would bring a special delivery, when our baby chicks we raised every year came in the mail. Can you believe that?

What I was really looking for those summer days was a letter from Roy Rogers, one of the famous singing cowboys in the movies. In the Sunday paper a couple of weeks earlier there had been a contest explaining that Trigger, his horse, and Trigger's wife were going to have a baby colt, and Roy Rogers was going to give someone $500 to come up with its name. We had an old horse named Pompy, and I thought that would be a great name for his new colt, so I entered the contest. I knew no one else would enter that name and was sure I would win the contest. Dad gave me two or three cents to mail it, and I was waiting for the letter every day, but Roy Rogers hadn't answered me yet. That was really the letter I was hoping would come in the mail, but as I read what kind of mail we got, and most of it was junk or magazines, I got all excited because there was a letter from my sister Myrtle.

I took the letter to Dad who opened it. Myrtle had written that she, Stanley, and the three kids were coming home for the weekend and that Stanley wanted to go fishing! This was terrific news! I ran outside to look for Wendell, Roger, and Gayle and told them that Stanley was coming Friday and we were to get everything ready to go fishing!

Going fishing when I was growing up was a big deal and a common occurrence, though it wasn't usually like the fishing you might imagine.

About three to four miles from our Home Place was the Grand River. It was located about one mile south of Pattonsburg. There is a sign in New Pattonsburg – the town of "old" Pattonsburg was relocated after a series of floods – that says, "The best catfish fishing in the world." That may very well be true.

Later in life, my brothers Miles, Johnny, Roger, Gayle, and I went many times during reunions to the Grand River and fished for catfish with fishing poles, catching quite a few. The catfish were the perfect size to eat, weighing about one to two pounds each. Each time we would catch about ten to fifteen fish in about two hours and call it a day. A couple of times we skinned them and fried them on the spot, and they were delicious. A couple of times we gave them away to friends because we didn't have the time or the desire to skin them and eat them, and our friends were always happy to get a good fresh meal of catfish.

I call that normal, modern day fishing.

Miles, Johnny, and Gayle were good at normal pole fishing, and Roger and I usually just went along for the camaraderie. The bait we used to catch those fish was canned "stink bait" purchased somewhere nearby. Miles, Johnny, and Gayle probably had about $200 worth of rods and reels, hooks, and who knows what all they had in their tackle boxes. Roger and I just borrowed from them and got the equipment they didn't like, but we didn't care and were lucky if we caught one fish. I really didn't know what I was doing anyway.

To tell you the truth, those fishing exercises were what we call modern fishing minus the $30,000 fishing boat and trailer and the $30,000 truck to haul it to a big lake, where it takes all day, and most are lucky to catch half as many fish, even with a tackle box as big as a small truck and $500 worth of fancy lures and stuff. At least we were fishing in a river, which is a lot less effort and a real fishing experience, and we had a lot of fun doing that together.

Wendell was the real fisherman in the family, and he fished a lot in Grand River, so I pestered him all day if I could help him get everything organized for our fishing expedition with Stanley, and he finally said I could. I could hardly shut up about it and didn't sleep well that night thinking. When we got up Thursday morning he told me to go to the garage and take down all the trotlines we had that were hung on the north side of the inside of the garage. When I got them there were five.

Now I imagine you might be thinking, "What the heck is a trotline?" Well a trotline is a heavy fishing line attached at about two foot intervals with branch lines hanging down from the main line, with a fishing hook at the end of each branch. The main line is around fifty feet long with about twenty-five branch lines attached. Most purchased trotlines have the branch lines attached with a clip or a swivel. But Wendell made his trotlines himself and couldn't afford to buy those swivels, so his were attached with a special knot he had learned to use. I learned that knot when I was a Scoutmaster for the Boy Scouts many years later in Greenfield, Missouri. I guess Wendell learned the knot from the older brothers or from Dad. The name of that knot was a square knot or what the Scouts called a double half hitch.

To catch a fine mess of catfish, you would tie a simple overhand knot when tying the ends of a baited trotline to a tree or root of a fallen tree at the edge of the river, someplace where it would be easily untied when removing the trotline and taking it home to store in the garage. When I took the five trotlines to Wendell to examine, he said they were all in good shape except that a few of the hooks were missing and that he would tie new ones on. He said five were plenty for what we would need over the coming weekend.

The reason those hooks needed to be tied on properly was when a two to five pound catfish was hooked it would fight like crazy and try to get that hook out of its mouth and get away before we would pull the lines out of the water. Wendell was going to make sure that knot was tied properly so that a strong fighting fish wouldn't pull the trotline off the tree or tree stump. So step one was completed in preparation for fishing with Stanley.

Now Wendell was ready for step two. He told me to go get the seine out of the garage. If you don't know what a seine is, then I will tell you. If you have read the Christian Bible you will remember that some of Jesus's disciples were fishermen who initially could catch nothing, and Jesus told them to put their seine into the water and it would be full of fish. A seine is a net that we used to put in our pond water, letting it settle for a while at the bottom of the pond, to catch crawfish or crawdads, that's what we called them. They sort of look like little lobsters. I never did know why there were literally thousands of crawdads in our pond.

Our seine had a pole on each end of the net that two of us boys, usually Gayle and I, would grab ahold of, and we would wade into the shallow pond, dragging the front pole forward and going about ten feet, letting the net settle, then circling back to shore and lifting the seine out of the water. Each time we did this we'd have as many as fifty crawfish caught in the seine, and we would dump them into a metal bucket with a lid on it until we had 150-200 crawdads, and that was our bait for catching catfish.

When I took the seine to Wendell he commented that it was old and in pretty bad condition. It was rolled up, and when he unrolled it there were a couple of holes in it, and he said we couldn't catch crawdads in that. He went into the house and came back with a large darning needle and heavy string and sewed up those holes. It was really neat how he did that saying, "That will do fine."

Now we were ready for step three. Wendell took the seine and put it in the garage with the trotlines and said, "The minnow bucket should be in here but it isn't. You and Gayle go find it. It should have been put in here with this other fishing stuff the last time we went fishing, but it isn't. I have no idea where it is, you will just have to look for it." The name for that metal bucket with the lid on it was called the minnow bucket because it was made to put minnows in when people would go pole fishing, but we didn't even have fishing poles at that time that I can remember, though the bucket worked just fine for crawdads too. He said, "See that large nail on the wall by the trotlines, that's where the minnow bucket should have been put," adding, "and when you find it take it to the well, put a couple of inches of water in it, and bring it to me."

Gayle and I looked for that minnow bucket for an hour. We looked in the barn but it wasn't there. We looked on the front porch but it wasn't there. We asked Dad if he knew where it was but he didn't know either. Then all of a sudden I remembered and told Gayle, "You know, I think I remember seeing it in the cellar." We opened the door and, sure enough, there it was sitting on the shelf on the south side of the cellar. In addition to food, we kept a lot of tools such as axes, hoes, wood wedges, and sledge hammers there. There was also a posthole digger, a hammer, and twisted binding wire hanging on nails. There was a washtub full of gunny sacks and a roll of barbed wire and other stuff like that, but the minnow bucket seemed strangely out of place. Anyway, Gayle told me to take it to the well and pump a little water and take it to Wendell. When I got back, Dad came out to meet me and announced that lunch – we called it dinner – was ready, and he told me to go get Wendell and Roger and tell them.

When dinner was over and we went back outside to do our afternoon work, Wendell asked me where the minnow bucket was. I got it and took it to him. He looked at it and said, "Good, the bucket doesn't have any holes in it because the water is still in it, so it will be fine to put the crawdads in and they won't die. Hang this up in the garage with the trotlines where it belongs."

Step three was done, so now we were ready for step four. Wendell told me to find at least two stringers to put fish on when we would take them off the trotlines. I figured they were in the garage but didn't see them anywhere. A fish stringer is a line of wire or a chain with large clasps that can be pushed to open and close to secure the fish we caught. The fish can be hooked by their gills so they can be immersed in water without getting loose but kept alive. If we would have had a tackle box, then it would have been in there, but we didn't have a tackle box. That cost money, and Dad did not spend money on things such as that. It took me about fifteen minutes, but I finally found them in the bottom of a cardboard box that contained some lead weights, some extra hooks, and other miscellaneous items we might need for fishing or repairing our fishing gear. I took the entire box to the barn and found Wendell in the corn crib, where he and Roger were putting whole corn, cobb and all, in a couple of bushel baskets to feed to the pigs. I told him I had found a couple of stringers and asked if there was anything else in the box we would need? He looked at the stringers and said they were ok. He picked out of the box a pair of snub-nosed plyers and a rusty pair of scissors, though the scissors he determined were unsatisfactory. He told me to get an empty cigar box – and there were several in the garage that we kept to put things in just for situations like this – so our items wouldn't get lost. So we put the pliers and all of the fish hooks in the cigar box, then put that box with the other fishing gear we were putting together.

Wendell then told me to take the rusty scissors to Dad to see if he would sharpen them. I took them to Dad, finding him in the garden digging some potatoes. I told him Wendell wanted to know if he could sharpen the scissors because he thought he would need them for fishing with Stanley. Dad said he would in a while, asking me to go to the porch and wait for him. I did that, but I waited for what seemed like quite a while, probably twenty minutes, when he finally did show up with a bucket of potatoes. Dad went into the house and came out with a gray stone of some kind, and then he took the scissors and started rubbing the blades on the stone. He did a funny thing though: he spit on the stone before he started. I asked him why he did that, and he just said he would tell me later. I asked him what that gray rock was, and he told me it was called a whetstone. A whetstone is used to sharpen things like a pocket knife, but it could be used to sharpen other things as well. I enjoyed watching him do what he was doing, but it took a while. Pretty soon, the rusty cutting edges became shinier. He had to do both blades on each side, and he was done in about twenty minutes. He then told me to go to the garage and get him the hand held oil can and bring it to him. I did this, and he squirted a little oil all over the rusty scissors and, with an old piece of cloth, rubbed the oil in the scissors. He then told me to put them in the garage, still a little wet with oil, with the trotlines. He explained to me the reason for oiling the scissors. He said the scissors would now open and close easier and cut much better after setting for a couple of days. I asked Dad why scissors were called a pair of scissors, when there was really only one, and he said because there were two blades. Scissors wouldn't cut if there was only one blade.

I went back to Wendell and told him what Dad had done, and he nodded as if he already knew. He told me not to forget to put the scissors in the cigar box with the other stuff for Saturday morning. He said, "Tomorrow morning we will take the trotlines, string them out in the front yard, and replace any hooks that are missing or rusty, because the hooks need to be sharp."

Step four was completed, and we would start on step five tomorrow, which would be Friday. I was really getting excited. Myrtle and Stanley would arrive about four or five in the afternoon. I thought to myself that Wendell was smart and efficient to get everything ready to go fishing before Stanley got here. What he was doing was going to save a lot of time.

Friday morning came and the first thing I thought of was fishing. I bounced out of bed along with everybody else at 5:00 a.m. as usual. I went outside to do my chores while everyone else did their chores. They had to get the cows in from the pasture. Sometimes the cows would already be around the barn, so my brothers wouldn't have to go get them and herd them in, but not today. Meanwhile Dad was preparing breakfast, and Gayle had gone to the well for Dad to get a three gallon pail of water to start the day.

I was at the woodpile picking up some kindling to get the kitchen stove going. The kindling we used consisted of small slivers of wood, a few corncobs, and even some tree bark. There was always some kindling and small pieces of firewood behind the kitchen stove, and what I was bringing in was keeping the kindling box full and dry. Then I went back to the woodpile and brought in some small split firewood. I brought my two arms full to restock the firewood so there would always be plenty that was dry, along with the dry kindling, behind the stove. Then I went to the hen house and gathered freshly laid eggs, bringing them in. Then I stayed in the house and took off my coat and gloves. I always wore gloves when picking up kindling and firewood to prevent getting splinters in my hands. Such was our normal, early morning routine.

I now washed my hands and face and set the table for breakfast, getting the milk and butter out of the refrigerator. Our new refrigerator was nice because not too long ago we had an old icebox, and it just didn't keep things as long without the food and milk spoiling.

Breakfast was our biggest meal on the farm. We would have bacon or sausage and once in a while ham, biscuits and gravy, eggs and toast, jams and jellies, cereal or oatmeal, and maybe some canned fruit from the cellar. There was always fresh cream for the fruit and cereal. We always had a crock of milk in the refrigerator that had a thick layer of cream on top. We would skim off the cream for use at the table.

Just when breakfast was ready, here comes everybody from doing their chores. We would wash up and sit down for breakfast before starting out to do our daily jobs assigned by Dad. Dad was always good at giving all of us jobs to do, and I really didn't mind work as long as it was doing something I felt I could do well. I benefited greatly from that as I got older. This day all of us were to work in the garden. I was to thin out the beets and carrots, which was a tedious job but not hard to do, and since I was low to the ground that was a job I generally got. The other guys had to hoe and chop small weeds and maybe spray some of the plants for bugs. They might have to dig a few potatoes, pick and hull some peas, pick some lettuce, or cut a head of cabbage to make slaw for our dinner meal. I had already bugged Wendell about fixing the trotlines, but he told me to cool it: that would have to wait until after dinner. We all worked pretty hard that morning, time went by pretty fast, and then Dad called us in for dinner. We had ham and beans, cornbread and slaw. We always had iced tea to drink. Dad used to buy a case of 7-Up soda every week that he dished out when he saw fit, as it had to last a week. Dad liked 7-Up too.

After dinner Wendell said, "We need to make some stakes to tie our trotlines to when we put them in the river in case there isn't something to tie them onto." He took an ax outside, cut down a sapling, and then made three stakes about three feet long each, putting them in the garage with the other stuff. While he was there he took the trotlines down and we carried them to the front yard and strung them out on the ground about four to five feet apart, checking all the small lines coming off the main line to make sure they were in good shape. If the lines had to be replaced, then Roger would cut some extra string about two foot long off a roll of string with those scissors Dad had cleaned and sharpened. They weren't oily and they cut great. Wendell would then tie them on. We did this with every trotline until they were all repaired. This took about an hour. Then Wendell started that same process with the hooks on every line, replacing those that were missing plus putting them on the strings we had just added. Of course he had to tie all those hooks on also. Roger was in charge of handing Wendell hooks as he needed them.

Step five was finally over. Those lines were ready to take to the river. Now we were ready for step six: the final step.

We got the minnow bucket and the seine out of the garage and took off for the pond that was about ten minutes away. When we got to the pond, which was pretty muddy and not clear at all, Gayle and I took off our shoes and socks, rolled up our pant legs, and each took one end of the seine and waded into the pond. Dropping the seine at an angle, we went in about ten feet, made a circle, came back, lifted our seine, and there was a ton of crawdads. We repeated this process five or six times and our minnow bucket was almost full. We had all the crawdads we needed to bait all our hooks and have plenty left over. We went back to the house and put the crawdads – minnow bucket and all – in some water to keep them alive. Step six was over. We were ready to go to the river as soon as our visitors arrived.

There was one more thing we had left to do before Myrtle and Stanley's visit. We got out our lawn mower, which was the old type of push mower. You know, it was the sort of mower where you provided the power, not a motor. We proceeded to mow the grass down low and smooth for playing croquet. Stanley liked to play croquet. We set up the stakes and arches for a regulation court and brought out the croquet set, and we were finally ready for them to show up with Sharon and the twin boys, Joe and Jerry.

Sure enough, they showed up about 4:45 p.m. and we had our normal greetings. It was always nice to see any of our brothers and sisters with their families. Stanley wanted to know what he could do to get us ready to go fishing.

We showed him what we had done and he couldn't believe it. He said, "Let me help unpack and change into some fishing clothes and I will be ready to go!" So we loaded everything in the car, and when he came out we took off to the river. We knew just where we were going, and we were soon at our favorite sand bank and fishing spot on the Grand River, and we had the place completely to ourselves. We had all taken a load from the car and had everything there. It was now about 6:00 p.m. so we started to work.

We unwrapped our first trotline and stretched it out on the riverbank. We got our crawdads and placed one on every hook. Wendell and Stanley took it down to the river just a few feet away, then decided where they would place all the trotlines across the river, which was not that wide and a perfect place for trotlines. Wendell took one end of the first trotline and started walking across the river. When he got to the other side he tied the line to the root of a fallen tree, tying it with one of his knots that he knew would be secure. He then asked me to bring one of the stakes he had made, walking to the other end of the trotline where Stanley was, tying that end to the stake with another knot, and pushing the trotline itself, bait and all, into the river bottom. The river itself was only about two to four feet deep at this particular location, and the trotline was now secure and in place.

While Wendell and Stanley were doing that, Roger and Gayle and I were unraveling the next line, stretching it out on the bank and baiting the lines. Stanley and Wendell took that, went down river about ten feet, and then repeated that same process, with Wendell always finding something to tie the trotline to on the far end. This second time he found a log on Stanley's side to tie it to and didn't need a stake. Wendell was careful to make certain the entire trotline was below the surface of the water, with the only thing visible being a stake top or a little bit of the main line. Everyone just repeated their job until all five trotlines were in the water and tied to something steady and strong.

Just so you know, dusk, night-time, and dawn are the best times to have trotlines out to catch fish.

That was it! We were now officially fishing.

We packed up all our remaining gear at dusk and drove home, where a delicious supper was waiting. After supper, and while we were actually fishing, we played cards, of course, visited until about 11:00 p.m., and then went back to the river to check our trotlines.

That was always an anxious time, wondering if there were any fish on the lines, but normally there would be some, but we never knew just how many.

Parking our car maybe three or four hundred yards from our fishing spot in the dark, we had to go through a lot of underbrush and cross several fences, but Wendell knew exactly where to go because he had fished this spot in the river many times.

We had a couple of flashlights to show the way to our fishing spot. We got there with our bait, stringers, a few extra hooks, and a pocket knife. Wendell would first pull on one of the trotlines. If there were hooked fish on the line, then he would feel them tugging, and then Wendell would say, "Oh yeah, there is something on this line!" He would then walk in the river to each hook until he came to where a fish was struggling, and he would say, "Boy, it's a nice one!" He would then ask me for the stringer, put the full palm of his hand on the belly of the catfish to calm it down, and then grab it by its fins. I would unclasp a hook on the stringer, and he would hook the fish by the gills and clasp the hook shut. Wendell would then take the fish hook out of its mouth and move on down the line. There may be more on that line.

So we would move on down the line. Roger and Gayle would follow us with the crawdad bucket, replacing any missing bait from a given hook. Bait could go missing for lots of reasons other than when a catfish had eaten our bait, hooked or not. Normally each trotline had about twenty-five baited hooks on it, and so it was not unusual to catch two or three fish. We would just go from line to line until all of the lines had been run. Sometimes you wouldn't catch any, but sometimes you might catch four or five per line. When my stringer would get full, usually with about eight fish, I would then take it to Stanley. He would dip the stringer of fish in the river every five minutes or so to keep them alive. I would then take another stringer and hope to fill it as well.

When we were done running the lines we would go back and lift the ones we had already run, and once in a while we would already have hooked another. If so, then we'd go get it, and then we'd go home. By then it was probably about 1:00 a.m., but before we could go to bed we had to skin the fish and put them in the refrigerator in salt water. Still fishing while we slept overnight, early the next morning, about 6:00 a.m., we went to run the lines again. We had caught about the same number, then returned home, put the fish in a tub to wash, skinned a couple, and then Myrtle fixed us all some fresh catfish for breakfast. After breakfast we skinned the rest of the fish, and then we ate delicious fish all weekend.

Then the tough decision: do we go back to the river and take the lines out, or do we do the same thing tonight? Now that is what I call FISHING!

EARLY CIVIL BEND AND THE GENERAL STORE

So what about Civil Bend itself? What little hamlet supported all of this farming, playing, hunting and fishing, and family life, and what is its forgotten history?

As the story goes, it was in 1849 that a certain Dr. J.W. Hightree, a recent medical graduate of Western Reserve College in Cleveland, Ohio, went adventuring. Born on May 25, 1825 in Trumbull County, Ohio, Dr. Hightree began practicing medicine at the age of twenty-one. Three years later, in 1849, he moved to Lee County, Iowa in a covered wagon with his wife and family, where he continued practicing medicine. In January 1857, however, he and his family decided to move on once again, with the intention of making Florida their destination, primarily on account of his wife's ill health.

On the way to Florida, however, Dr. Hightree and his wife stopped to rest in Daviess County, Missouri, and this proved to be their journey's end. Mrs. Hightree fell in love with the place and desired to make it their home. The doctor agreed, bought some land, and they began living in a log house. In the census of 1860, 1870, and 1880, Dr. Hightree was listed as a physician living in Daviess County, and his log house was still standing in 1937. In fact, this log house was also the first doctor's office in what came to be known as the Civil Bend area: a small village composed of civil individuals near a very pleasant bend in the nearby Grand River.

Dr. Hightree made good in his profession. He possessed a well-improved farm for that time, as well as a nice brick and wood home, and he passed away on January 22, 1892. His son William, the only remaining member of the family, remained living on the place when I was a young boy. William, always known as "Bill," and known as well to let goats roam freely about his house, kept in his possession the medical instruments his father used in his profession. Among them was a tooth pulling instrument that always gave me a creepy feeling, making me glad I lived in more modern times.

As the population of the area increased over the years, so did the need for a General Store. In 1860, a gentleman by the name of John T. Price, a farmer in Harrison County, Missouri, near Trenton, decided to come to Daviess County with his wife and family. At that time, Mr. Price, who was listed as a farmer in the Daviess County census in 1860, was selling dry goods merchandise from house to house. He apparently decided sometime thereafter that a store would be a good investment, so he built a building for that purpose, completed about 1870. The first General Store in the area was said to be about sixteen feet square, perfectly adequate for those days.

John T. Price was born September 2, 1835, and he died May 30, 1901, murdered by his brother-in-law, Austin Miller.

The inland village of Civil Bend was laid out in 1868 by Gilbert Canfield, brother-in-law of Dr. Hightree, who surveyed the twenty-four lots from which the little village was started. Gilbert Canfield was born January 28, 1831 in Trumbull County, Ohio. He died July 06, 1883, and he is buried in the Civil Bend Methodist Cemetery, which lies between our farm and the Other Place.

Down through the years, from about 1860 to 1895, we find the following names connected with the business life of the Civil Bend community: Orlando (Buddy) Price, dealer in general merchandise; Peniston and Roberts, dealers in general merchandise; O.F. Schumway, druggist; Martin Smith, harness maker; Fred Snider, S.S. Ryan, and Joe Duffey, blacksmiths; Mose Mallory, shoemaker; R. Davis, barber; Ike Henderson, General Store proprietor; Col. J.T. Lee, auctioneer; S.L. Hardinger, doctor; and those who ran the Mutual Telephone Company.

JOHN HAVER, FATHER OF MINNIE OLIVE HAVER, MY GRANDMOTHER

There were two active churches in the early days of Civil Bend: the M.E. Methodist Church and the Christian Church. The Methodist Church was where I and my family went to church every Sunday, unless we were sick or unable to attend for some reason. The charter members of the original church, dedicated on April 1, 1868, were many of our ancestors. They included our great, great grandparents, James and Joannah Haver, the original purchasers of the Other Place. Later members would include our great grandparents, John William Haver and Mary Elizabeth Frazier, my grandfather, John H. Johnson, and our grandmother, Minnie Olive Haver. The board of trustees included our great grandfather and our grandfather.

At one time the I.O.O.F. and Masonic lodges were important and active in Civil Bend. Some members moved away, and some deaths caused a decrease in membership. Both lodges eventually passed into history, and the people here who wished to join either organization had to go to Pattonsburg or Gallatin.

N.B. Brown passed away in 1935, the year before I was born. He was very active in early Civil Bend history, had an extensive knowledge of the law, and was often chosen as a legal advisor in lawsuits in the early days. He was the father of Frank Brown, the man who ran the Central Office with his wife Bertie when I was a kid.

The DeKalb County Mutual Telephone Company sold out to the Civil Bend Company in 1911, which was incorporated in 1912. One of the directors of the Civil Bend Company was my great uncle, Harvey Haver, and Frank and Bertie Brown ran the business right across from the General Store.

A post office was put in the back of Ike Henderson's General Store around 1895. Ike and his wife later moved to Pattonsburg, where he engaged in the same business, though he maintained his store in Civil Bend for several more years, for a time in partnership with my grandfather Othniel Bruner, Jr., and later managed by John Cope. The 1900 census shows that Orlando (Buddy) Price and his brother Frank were running the store, but the 1910 census shows that Orlando was then living in Harrison County, Missouri. In the meantime, Ike had sold his businesses in Pattonsburg and Civil Bend, and the new owner of the Civil Bend General Store became Martin Smith, who used to own the harness shop. He in turn sold it to Mr. and Mrs. Fred Canfield, who established a new store in 1907. Fred then sold the store to Chrisy Reno in 1917, and he operated the General Store that I remember into the mid-1940s.

The General Store was really something, featuring a full line of groceries, dry goods, feeds, flour, hardware, and notions. Mr. Reno also bought and sold cream and eggs. Gasoline and oil was sold there also. He operated the store for almost thirty years, and he was highly regarded for his fair and honorable dealings.

Mr. Reno was born and reared in the Civil Bend community and, therefore, like the rest of us in that town, was no stranger. The citizens were very proud of their General Store, which by then had been in existence for about seventy years, and the Reno store carried on the store tradition in just the way the pioneers would have it: it was a good place to trade, and every day they were open for business.

A gentleman named Perry operated the General Store in the mid-forties into the early 1950s but was not very successful, and then the store lay empty for several years, finally being razed in 1972 to make way for the new Interstate 35 highway that also went right through my Dad's property.

THE OTHER PLACE

There was hardly a day that went by on the farm that the phrase "the Other Place" was not spoken of or mentioned in conversation. So where was, and what was, this Other Place you have already heard so much about, and why was it so important to me, my family, and the community of Civil Bend?

The Other Place was a house and barn about a half mile from our own, as well as the land around it, just a bit further away from Civil Bend, and it was here that my father's mother, Minnie Olive Haver, was raised.

Our Home Place was where all of my fourteen brothers and sisters were born, save for Myrtle, and where all of them were raised. I guess you could say that was "our place," but that phrase was never used. Our house and the surrounding land was always referred to as "the Home Place," "our house," or "the place we grew up." The other house, which I will refer to as the Other Place for as long as I live, was a neat old house, now long gone, that did not seem at all like an old house to me. It was at least as big as our house, and it had a large wrap-around front porch. The house faced east, and that big porch stretched from the middle of the house all the way to the full length of the north side. I remember there was a large window on the east side under the porch with stained glass that was really cool.

It seemed odd to me that no one lived in that house that I can remember except my sister Georgia and her husband Earl, with their two children, and that was only for a short time. Bernice was their oldest child, about two years younger than me. I was her uncle when I was just two years old, and she was the first of my many nieces. Gene was the youngest child, I was four years older than him, and he was one of my many nephews. They lived there in the Other Place for about two or three years. Their last name was Bridgman.

We are going to do a little history about this house and the farmland it was built on, both before and after the Bruners entered the picture. Let's go back to where this all started.

According to the family history, on January 25, 1806, George Haver Jr. and wife Priscilla gave birth to a bouncing baby boy, James William, in Jefferson Township, Greene County, Pennsylvania. Priscilla's maiden name was Priscilla Pricey Villars, and James William was the sixth of seven children born to this union, all in Pennsylvania.

Our family descends on the maternal side from this James William Haver and his wife Joanna Murdock. We know that in 1864 James and Joanna, along with their children, which included an elder son named John, traveled by covered wagon from Pennsylvania to Missouri, ultimately landing in Civil Bend. There, James and Joanna purchased 140 acres of farmland in sections between 1864 and 1869 for $1,275, becoming the owners of the land we came to call the Other Place. In the meantime, their son John married Mary Elizabeth Frazier, and James, his father, continued to buy more land into the 1870s, increasing his holdings to 180 acres.

James and Joanna built their beautiful house on that farmland in 1864, and, according to the 1870 census, Minnie Olive Haver, John and Mary's daughter and my grandmother, was three years old. Mary and John eventually had three children: one son, Harvey, one daughter, Minnie Olive, our future grandmother, and one daughter who died in infancy. When Mary and John reached old age, they gave their only son, Harvey, the entire farm left to them by James. Harvey, to make the inheritance fair, was to pay his only sister, Minnie Olive, $11,500, and this was all accomplished in 1886. This is also the time the Bruners came into the picture as far as the Other Place and our Home Place is concerned.

Minnie Olive Haver had eloped, at the age of fifteen, to Oklahoma with her Sunday school teacher, my grandfather, Othniel Bruner, Jr., aged twenty-eight, in 1883, just three years before her inheritance. Minnie and Othniel Jr. were married at Vinita, Oklahoma on December 24. They then settled in Monrovia, Kansas, where Othniel Jr. was a teacher for three years, and a son, Haver, was born there on January 1, 1886. They returned to Civil Bend that same year, and John Haver, Minnie's father, went out to Kansas to help them move back.

Minnie, her father John, and infant son Haver traveled back to Missouri in a covered wagon. The reason they moved back was that Othniel Jr. had already moved to Civil Bend, having entered into a business deal with his friend Ike Henderson. Together, they operated the General Store in Civil Bend for several years, and the store was successful. A deed to what eventually became our Home Place was dated September 1886, showing that Othniel Jr. purchased a small farm of thirty-nine acres that year for $1200 from Seth and Elza Rulon. This thirty-nine acres adjoined the larger farm of James Haver, Minnie's grandfather.

Apparently, a log house already existed on this newly purchased land, and a two-story frame house addition was made around this time. It also appears that Othniel Jr. and Minnie originally lived in the two room log house with the addition with their first children.

MINNIE AND OTHNIEL, JR, RECENTLY MARRIED, CIRCA 1885

After Minnie had her second child, Virgil, in 1888, she was staying in John and Elizabeth Haver's house at the Other Place, recovering, when it burned to the ground. Everyone got out safely, but the home was a total loss. John and his father, James, were out in the fields, and Othniel was at his store in Civil Bend, and by the time they got there it was too late to save anything.

Virgil was born June 20, and the fire was very soon after that. Haver, Othniel and Minnie's first born son, said in his book *Mr. Broadwater* that even though he was only two and a half years old he remembered that!

At this time, according to a deed on record, Othniel Jr. and Minnie purchased one square acre of land from the Civil Bend Methodist church for $50. This land was right across the road from the Methodist cemetery, where most of the Havers and many of the Bruners are buried. It is where I go today to visit my deceased relatives. That square acre was purchased back in 1868 by members of the old Methodist Episcopal Church to build a new church on. That church was built, but it was too small. The congregation outgrew it very fast, and the new Methodist church was built in the town of Civil Bend about 1888.

Guess whose name was on that 1868 deed as the representative of that Methodist Episcopal Church authorizing the purchase of that one square acre? None other than John Haver, who was a board member of that church, the father of our grandmother Minnie Haver Bruner. This was the very same John Haver who was the son of the original owner of the Other Place.

Guess whose name was on the 1888 deed, twenty years later, representing the new Methodist Church, authorizing the sale of this same acre to Othniel and Minnie Bruner? You guessed it: the same John Haver, who was a trustee and board member of the new church too. Records show his signature on both deeds. Haver Bruner said in his *Mr. Broadwater* that his grandfather, John Haver, was Superintendent of the Civil Bend Church for many years.

THE NEW METHODIST EPISCOPAL CHURCH IN CIVIL BEND, CIRCA 1960

Othniel Jr. and Minnie now owned forty acres of land, and they had another child, Homer Russell, my father, born in 1890 in the log house on the Home Place. By early 1891, John and Mary Haver, having lost their old abode to the fire, were residing in their newly built home with James W. Haver due to the latter's bad health. Remember, James William was the one who started this whole story, as he was the first in our family line to own the Other Place, and he died on March 27, 1891.

The next year, in 1892, Othniel Jr. and family moved to the town of Civil Bend while a new house was built to replace the old log cabin and add on, along with a new barn. In 1893, Othniel Jr. and Minnie purchased another five acres of land for $100 from James and Mae Betts, which brought their total land holdings to forty-five acres. On April 8, 1894, Othniel and Minnie had their last son, Paul. He was born while they were temporarily living above the General Store. The new house and barn were finally finished in 1896, and Othniel and family moved into that new house: our Home Place.

Tragically, though, Othniel Bruner Jr., my grandfather, soon thereafter scandalously ran off with another one of his young Sunday school students at the church, this time only fourteen years old, abandoning our grandmother Minnie and their four boys, apparently never to be heard from again.

While I will return to my tragic grandfather, there are many stories, both serious and funny, that I should first recall from my early childhood related to the Other Place.

We used to do a lot of work on the Other Place, for example, particularly at the barn. It was really a well-built barn in very good condition. In some ways it was a better barn than the one at the Home Place, and it had to have been built at least thirty to forty years before ours. It was about fifty yards west of a well. My brother Gayle almost fell in that well when he was very young, probably five or six. Luckily, he fell between two loose boards and his arms kept him from falling through. That was a deep well, and a fall that far could have killed him. I think it was my brother Johnny that rescued him.

There were two sturdy sides of the barn: the east and the west. Dividing these two sides was an opening you could drive a team of mules through with a wagon full of loose hay. In the good old days there was a fork-lift that would come down over the wagon full of hay and grab a nice chunk. There was a pulley system where a horse would pull on a rope and lift the hay up to the loft, and then someone in the loft would release it, stack it up there, and then repeat that process until the load of hay was in the loft.

Just after Minnie and Othniel moved into their newly built home, and going through the process of putting up hay in their new barn, a scary incident occurred involving my father, still then a very young boy. The grownups were putting up hay using the new fork-lift pulley system, and my father was playing with his brother Haver in the hay. Somehow Russell got his hand caught up in the pulley rope, but Haver yelled as loud as he could and the horse pulling the rope fortunately stopped. Had it not, my father very possibly could have lost his hand as a young boy. That is yet another example of the dangers always lurking when growing up on a working farm.

Regarding the nice barn at the Other Place, the loft was on its east side, and that loft was huge. It was the full length of the barn north to south, about sixty feet or so, and about twenty-five feet wide east to west. That would hold a lot of hay.

Below the loft was a large open area where you could put the cows to feed them and keep them out of the cold in the wintertime. As I remember it, the floor of that loft was also in really good condition. Notice that I said this all happened in the good old days. By the time I was six or seven the pulley system wasn't working any more, and the hay was transferred from the wagon to the loft with pitchforks. We just lifted the hay by muscle to the loft, and some of that hay would always fall back down onto those doing the lifting.

This was a sweaty job, and the hay, especially the Lespedeza, which had a lot of little leaves, would stick to your skin and get really itchy. It was not fun, and it was hard work. The two guys in the loft didn't have it much easier than the one doing the lifting. It would get pretty hot and sweaty up there too. Lucky me, when I was old enough we didn't do that anymore because we didn't have that many cows or that many brothers or that many horses to do that.

The west side of the barn was about the same size as the loft side, but it was divided into sections where individual cows could be put in to calve, or give birth. They could be milked there also. The newborn calves could be kept in there to suckle until old enough to be separated from their mother and put out to pasture. There were water containers as well, as the water had to be carried by hand from the well for them to drink. Hay would be put in there also for the cows to eat, and straw kept from threshing was used for their bedding.

There was a loft above, just like on the other side of the barn, but we didn't use that loft for some reason. Maybe the flooring was in bad shape on that side. Those stanchions or sections could be used for various things. One, for example, would be a good place to put a castrated young bull, called a steer, to fatten up for butchering. Anyway, we continued to use the Other Place as if it were an extension of the Home Place.

OLD ONE EYE

When I was very small I can remember laying outside in the yard on blankets in the grass, just after dark, with my brothers Joe Dean, Johnny, Wendell, Roger, and Gayle. That was the only way we could keep cool in the hot summer evenings, and since Joe Dean was there I could not have been older than four.

Whenever we were out at night in the yard my brothers would tell stories. Some were true and some were made up, but when you are young and impressionable you often can't tell the difference. I would go out there every summer with my brothers, and until I was probably twelve years old I was pretty gullible, watching falling stars and constellations and the moon shining. It was a perfect time for the older boys to tell scary stories.

One night Wendell, who was the oldest one there and I was probably eight or ten years old, told us a story about Old One Eye.

According to Wendell, Old One Eye was a scary man who hung around the now abandoned Other Place, particularly at night. If you kept an eye out, Wendell said, then you might catch him watching from the upstairs window on the north side of the house, looking out for naughty boys. Wendell never did tell us exactly what Old One Eye looked like, but I always pictured him as a monster with one eye in the middle of his head. When I got older and read Homer's *Odyssey*, it reminded me of when Odysseus was locked in the cave with a giant Cyclops that ate four of his men before he escaped. I didn't think of Old One Eye as a giant, but I sure never did want to meet up with him. I also knew another thing for sure: I didn't ever want to go to the house at the Other Place at night by myself.

One night when we were out there in the yard, Wendell told me another story. I didn't yet know it, but in the graveyard up the road from us on the way to the Other Place, he was sorry to say but thought I should know for my own good, was the Lady With The Golden Arm. She would come out of her grave at night, also looking for little boys that didn't behave. He told me he thought Old One Eye and the Lady With The Golden Arm were in cahoots, so I had better behave, or they might catch me if I was bad. So check that off your list. Don't go past the cemetery or the Other Place at night.

One day Wendell and I were working at a pond that Miles had built just north of and across the road from the Other Place. It was the very same pond where I would later teach myself to swim. I can't remember what we were doing there, but all of a sudden Wendell yelled, "Oh my gosh, did you see that?!" I said, "See what?" He said, "I just saw Old One Eye in that window upstairs across the street looking out at us!" Scared, I looked for a long time at the window but didn't see anything. After a while we reluctantly went back to doing whatever we were doing and Wendell said, "Oh my gosh! There he is again!" I turned quickly to look, but I had missed him again. Now I was really scared, and I kept looking back up at that window until we left. Wendell or I never did see him again, thank goodness, and Wendell told me not to worry. He would never let Old One Eye get me as long as he was around.

Well, about this time of my young life, we pulled our onions out of the ground when they were ready to harvest, took them to the Other Place, and then put them on the upstairs floor to dry. We would put them on paper to keep things even drier, and then we'd get a few of them when needed. One night after supper, about two or three weeks after Wendell had seen Old One Eye, Dad came in the living room and told us he needed some onions. One of us needed to go to the Other Place, go upstairs, and get him some onions. He left a small sack on the table and went back to the kitchen.

Roger and Gayle went into the parlor to play a game. Pretty soon Wendell said, "Lee Roy, you are old enough to do that, you go get some onions. You know where they are." I told him I didn't want to go. It was dark. He told me I was too old to be afraid of the dark. He gave me a flashlight and told me to go before Dad got mad.

Well, I very reluctantly took off, and quite frankly I was more than a little afraid. Was I a good enough boy to be safe? I started up the road towards the cemetery, thinking about the Lady With The Golden Arm. When I got close to the graveyard I started running as fast as I could, but the graveyard was on the corner, and I had to run uphill past its west side, turn the corner, and then run down the hill, past the south side. I was really running fast. When I got to the bottom of the hill I felt better, as there was no sign of the ghost, but then, about 300 yards ahead, was the Other Place. Then I remembered Old One Eye.

I was really scared now, so I turned on the flashlight, walked to the lane of the Other Place, ran really fast up to the house, quickly opened the door, ran across the front room and up the stairs like a flash, got to the top, dropped the flashlight, panicked, but it didn't break, picked it up, ran to the back room where the onions were, grabbed three or four of them, flew down the stairs, and ran out of the house. Relief!

Oh, but I didn't get very far down the lane before realizing that in my haste I hadn't shut the door to the house! What a mistake! Now I had to go back and shut it, which I did lightning quick, then took off running down the lane, still scared to death, onto the road past the north side of the house and looked up at that window, where I was sure I saw a glowing red light. Then I just kept running as fast as I could.

I thought, boy I was lucky. I just kept running with my onions and then thought, oh no, I've got to run past the graveyard again! I stood there for probably a full minute building up the courage and thought, heck, I have no choice. So I put my feet into high gear and ran up the hill past the graveyard, turned the corner, and ran all the way home.

When I finally got back to the house I collected myself and acted cool. I put the onions on the kitchen table, turned the flashlight off, put it on the table as well, and Dad said, "That was fast. Why did you only get three onions? You should have got at least six or so." Momentarily horrified, thinking he might want me to go back, I quickly said, "I didn't know how many to get, but I will be sure to get more the next time."

When I went in the living room Wendell said, "Did you find the onions?" I said, "Yep, sure did."

OTHNIEL BRUNER JR.

I want to say more about my grandfather, Othniel Bruner Jr.

My grandfather was a school teacher, a licensed minister in the Methodist church, and fairly well-educated for his time, though his life was ultimately a tragic one.

OTHNIEL BRUNER, JR., MY GRANDFATHER

Some facts we do know for sure about my grandfather. He was born March 31, 1855, somewhere in Indiana. He was the third of nine children born to Othniel Bruner, Sr., a Methodist minister, and Antis Blair Bailiff.

In 1860, at age five, Othniel Jr. was living with his parents and two brothers in Mattoon Township, Coles County, Illinois. In 1870, at age fifteen, he was living with his parents and four siblings in Noble Township, Richland County, Illinois. In 1880, at the age of 25, he was apparently still living with his parents and three siblings in Colfax Township, Daviess County, Missouri, very likely in the town of Winston, Missouri, where Othniel Sr. served as a Methodist-Episcopal minister.

Othniel Jr. worked as a painter in Winston, while one of his brothers, Morris, worked as a painter in Maysville, Dekalb County, Missouri. Maysville is about the same distance from Civil Bend as Winston, so there is a good chance they may have painted together at times.

We also have records indicating that Othneil Jr. and his brother Morris attended Asbury University, now DePauw University, in Greencastle, Indiana in 1876, but they did not complete their degrees. How long they were in college we do not know; however, we do know that Othniel Jr. was a charter member of the Beta Beta Chapter of the Delta Tau Delta Fraternity. The Fraternity includes a date of 1880 next to his name in their records.

Before I get into the Bruner family story, I feel I need to provide a bit more insight into, and history of, Dad's mother, Minnie Olive Haver.

Our grandmother, Minnie Olive, was born December 16, 1867. Her father was John William Haver, born June 20, 1840, and her mother was Mary Elizabeth Frazier - Haver. At the age of thirteen Minnie became a member of the Civil Bend Methodist Church at Civil Bend Missouri, and she remained a member the rest of her life, taking an active part in the church and her community as long as her health permitted. She taught a Sunday school class when she was 82 years of age, and she was a Sunday school teacher for over fifty years. She remained patient and cheerful during her latter days of illness.

As a kid, as early as I can remember, the entire family went to church and Sunday school every Sunday. We attended the small Methodist church in Civil Bend. I think it was just as much a social event as a religious event for everyone, including Dad, but I was too young to realize that. Attending church and Sunday school continued until I left home.

Dad was a prominent figure in the church. I remember him going early Sunday morning around 8:00 a.m. to start the fire in the church furnace so the sanctuary would be warm. Church started at 10:00 a.m., and he was the church's treasurer forever, I think.

I am sure going to church and Sunday school was a good thing. I learned a little about Bible characters in Bible stories. I learned to sit still for an hour during church, which was very boring. The sermons, I thought, were pretty bad, and certainly of no interest to me. I did, though, memorize a lot of church songs that I would sing to myself while doing chores or adventuring.

I went to Bible school at the Civil Bend church every summer, and there might have been ten to fifteen other kids. I can't remember for sure. A few memorized Bible verses stick with me today, however. "Do unto others as you would have them do unto you." Also, "Love one another as your father in heaven loves you." A few of the beatitudes. I didn't get all my stars on my certificate because I only memorized four of the eight. Those two quotes are still basically my philosophy of life, as I have written several times in my journals. I attended church and Sunday school from birth to seventeen years of age on a regular basis. Even though I was taught a lot, I know what I believe. I was taught a lot I don't believe. I am glad I was exposed to God, though. When I grew up, I studied and researched for my own truth.

Anyway, back to my grandfather and his story. Minnie Olive, now age sixteen, married Othniel Jr., age twenty-eight, on December 24, 1883 in Vinita, Oklahoma, and they, as noted, eventually had four sons: Haver, Virgil, Homer Russell (my father), and Paul.

MINNIE OLIVE BRUNER AND HER CHILDREN: HAVER,
VIRGIL, RUSSELL, AND PAUL, CIRCA 1898

In a great tragedy for our family and its history, our grandfather ran off, leaving our grandmother and her four young children, on May 21, 1898.

According to Daviess County Court documents, eight years later, in April of 1906, a lawsuit was filed by Minnie against the Modern Woodmen of America insurance company. The reason for the lawsuit was to try and collect on a life insurance policy Othniel Jr. had with them. This led to some interesting revelations.

Documents from the lawsuit offer two very different explanations as to what became of our forty-three-year-old grandfather after leaving his family in 1898. In the court case, Minnie indicated that Othniel Jr. left his home and traveled to St. Joseph, in Buchanan County, Missouri. On May 22, 1898, he left a suitcase containing his belongings with a suicide note on a bridge over the Missouri River. Minnie then assumed he died by drowning after jumping from the bridge. A few days later a body was indeed recovered in Leavenworth, Kansas and buried there. Court documents mention newspaper articles reporting these facts. Documents also refer to the suicide note, which apparently was in the possession of our grandmother.

Attorneys for the Modern Woodmen of America, however, took depositions in early 1906 in Enid, Oklahoma, in the Oklahoma Territory (Oklahoma did not become a State until November 16, 1907) from a twenty-two year old woman, Gertrude Shaw, now married to Mr. Hugh Kelly, who claimed to have had a secret relationship in Civil Bend with Othniel Jr. prior to his disappearance. Gertrude's father, Clinton Shaw, was present and understandably very protective of his daughter. Gertrude's statements describe the following scenario:

Gertrude was asked how long she had known Othniel Jr., and she said they had known each other since she was ten years old. He was her Sunday school teacher. Several years later, Othniel and Gertrude, then fourteen, had a secret relationship prior to his leaving Daviess County. She knew before he left what he was going to do. They made plans, she said, for Othniel to leave the area and pretend to commit suicide. He would then assume the name of George W. Bayless and contact her by letter, addressed to Miss Maude Bayless, Pattonsburg, Missouri. There was a post office in Civil Bend in 1898, but she would have to pick the letter up at the post office in Pattonsburg to avoid suspicion.

Gertrude claimed she received two letters. She could not remember where they were sent from, but it was from a small town somewhere in southern Illinois. The letters were signed G.W.B., and she was told by Othniel Jr. to burn the letters. She received the letters around the first of June 1898. Othniel Jr. had also given her some money for train fare.

The gentleman doing the deposition asked Gertrude what type of agreement the two of them had. She said he would leave his clothes and a watch on a bridge near a town with a suicide note, leaving the impression he had jumped and drowned. He had made arrangements for her to contact the matron of Union Station in St. Louis, and she would provide her a place to stay, which she did. The two of them would meet up in the Union Depot in St. Louis and start a new life together.

Gertrude stated that she left her home on July 7 or 8 and stayed with her uncle in Altamont, Missouri in Daviess County. That was only about ten or fifteen miles from her home and on the way to St. Louis. I do not have any records on how she got to Altamont, but Gertrude left a letter with her uncle and aunt to be given to her parents, after she left Altamont, the next time they saw each other. She then took off for St. Louis but had to change cars in Kansas City, Missouri. She left Daviess County without the knowledge of her family, traveling by train. Shortly thereafter her aunt became suspicious, opened the letter, and her parents became aware of her plan. Her father tracked her down in St. Louis and returned with her to Daviess County without her having met up with Othniel. She said the last time she saw him was the day he left my grandmother. Minnie Olive never saw him again as far as we know.

Attorneys for the Modern Woodmen of America also presented depositions taken from two women who ran a boarding home in Marion, Illinois. These two women identified Othniel Jr. in a photograph, but they said they knew him by the name of Mr. Bayless. They stated that he had stayed at their boarding home on two occasions during the summer of 1898. He first arrived there in June or July and stayed about three weeks, but during this time he became sick with malaria and almost died. After he recovered, the aforementioned Mr. Bayless left for about a week, saying he was going to see a young girl who was under his care. He returned to the boarding home alone and stayed several more weeks, leaving for the last time in late August. The women said he did not appear to be well when he left, and they never saw him again.

The attorneys of the Modern Woodmen of America also took a statement from Gertrude's father, Clint Shaw, who condemned Othniel Jr. for the ravishing of his daughter.

Mr. Shaw was one of the wealthiest farmers in Daviess County, and when he returned from St. Louis with Gertrude he immediately went to the courthouse in Gallatin, Missouri, authorizing the county's sheriff to offer a substantial reward for Othniel Jr.'s capture.

Here is the article that appeared in the *St. Louis Republic* newspaper on July 20, 1898, page 11:

AFTER BRUNER: Big reward offered for the would-be abductor of a Gallatin girl. REPUBLIC SPECIAL.

Gallatin, Mo., July 19, 1898—Othniel Bruner, who left his home and family at Civil Bend, in this county, on May 21 and pretended to have jumped into the Missouri River at St. Joseph on May 23 leaving a note to that effect and his clothing on the bridge, has turned up alive and is a much wanted man by citizens residing in and near Civil Bend as a result of his recent attempt to abduct the 14 year old daughter of Clint Shaw, one of the wealthiest farmers in the county.

Mr. Shaw today deposited $500.00 in the Gallatin Savings Bank and authorized Daviess County's Sheriff to offer the sum as a reward for Bruner's capture. The sheriff has positive information that Othniel was alive on July 12, 1898 and was then in Johnson City, Williamson County, Illinois where Othniel had been located some days. Othniel sent a telegram from there to the police matron, Union Station, St. Louis on Friday, July 08 in the name of G.W. Bayless and while there received a letter addressed to him in the name of O.F. Lathrop. He left Johnson City on July 13, 1898 and went to Benton, Illinois, ostensibly on his way to St. Louis to meet the girl, who was to meet him at Union Station. There is talk of lynching him if he returns here.

There are two interesting points of possible coincidence. First, Othniel Jr. had lived in the town of Marion, Illinois sometime between the ages of five and fifteen, while his father served as a minister there. Second, his younger brother Joseph (aka John Edmond) was married in Marion on May 18, 1898, just three days before Othniel disappeared from Civil Bend.

The date of death and place of burial for Othniel Jr. are not known. There is some evidence, however, that he was deceased by June 16, 1900. The 1900 federal census record for his mother was made on that date, and she indicates she had given birth to nine children and only four remained living: Morris, Antis May, Josef (aka John Edmond) and Jency. These four individuals are all known to have died after 1912. Also, Othniel Jr.'s mother died in 1915, and her obituary indicated she was survived by only two of her children: her daughters. Still, she may have simply disowned him, given his tragic choices.

Minnie, who one can imagine went through a terrible ordeal in such a tight knit community, eventually remarried John H. Johnson of Civil Bend in 1910, living on to a ripe and pleasant old age, and all four of her children grew up to be honorable and respected persons and citizens.

STORIES RELATED TO MY SISTERS

Let's now return to the brighter aspects of life in Civil Bend with some stories about my sisters, which will tell you a lot about life at the Home Place. Let's start with my wonderful sister Carol.

I was five years old and my sister Carol and her husband Clifford Burton came after breakfast, picked me up, and took me in their car to their house for the day. I guess they had asked Dad if they could have me for a day or Dad may have asked them to take me for the day, I do not know. The latter may have been the case because they were putting electricity in our house that day. I did not know, though, that that was going to happen. I had been home a few days earlier when they put up the big pole outside and put lines to the house. I remember them putting the transformer on that pole, and I probably asked Dad a thousand questions. He probably thought I was in the way and didn't want me around pestering everybody. I really didn't understand what was going on.

They took me to their house, and, while I don't remember much of what we did that day, I liked Carol a lot and was always glad to go with her. After they fed me supper they took me home and it was dark. When we came over the hill at the Other Place I could see our house in the distance, and I was immediately frightened. I said to Carol, "Our house in on fire!" She said, "No, you got electricity in your house today!"

I was so excited that I couldn't wait to get home and go inside, and when we finally did I discovered that each room of the house had one light bulb in the middle of the ceiling. It was so light in the house I couldn't believe it! No more studying and reading at night with oil lamps for everyone. I couldn't wait to tell my teacher, Mrs. Foley, when I went to school the next day, but I can tell you now that it changed our lives on the farm forever.

Carol was involved in another important incident in my life when I was about twelve years old. It was a very hot summer day, and Dad took Gene Bridgman and me to St. Joseph, Missouri to visit my brother Homer, who owned a gasoline station and a 24 hour diner across town by the stock yards. He and his wife Dorothy lived above the gas station. We got to Homer and Dorothy's, visited for a while, and then had a sandwich for lunch. After lunch, Dad wanted to go to my sister Carol's house, which was also there in St. Joseph.

When we got to Carol's house and visited for a while, she suggested, because it was so hot, that Homer and Dad take Gene and I to a swimming pool just a short distance away. They did that, and, as we were getting into the pool, Dad told us not to venture off and to stay in the shallow end of the pool, since neither of us could swim. We agreed and jumped in. After a while, though, I wanted to get out because I had to pee. While looking for a bathroom, Gene said to me, "When I need to pee I just go in the pool." He was only five years old, and I should have known better, but I jumped back in the pool.

Well, without thinking, I had jumped into the other end of the pool and the water was eight feet deep there, and so I sunk to the bottom because I could not swim. There must not have been lifeguards at that pool back then. I was frantic and tried to swim but couldn't. I came up, but not for long, and then went under again. I was still trying to swim, and after another thirty seconds or so I came up again. This time, though, I went down again, and something very weird happened. My life passed before me!

I evidently was groping around and my hand finally brushed against something metal. I grabbed hold of it. It was a ladder, and I climbed out.

I told Gene not to tell Dad or Homer because they would just get angry, and I would probably get a spanking and have to leave. We never did tell them what happened. We went back to the shallow end of the pool and they never knew anything about it. I couldn't get out of my mind, though, what had happened to me in the pool, when my entire life passed before me. It was the strangest thing, and I never told Gene or anyone else about that for many years. I knew they would just say, "Aw, quit making stuff up."

Years later, when I was about forty years old, I called Gene. I told him I was taking a short trip back to Civil Bend and Pattonsburg to visit some old high school friends and asked if he would like to go with me. He said he would. A couple of days later we took off and traveled some of the side roads. Some roads we never had been on, and we went through towns we had never visited. It was a nice trip. We stopped in a little town called Tightwad, Missouri, and there we found a small diner that looked like a clean place to have lunch. While we were eating, I asked Gene if he remembered when he was five or six and I almost drowned. He said, "Heck yes, I will never forget that, I thought you were a goner." I asked him if he would describe what happened as he remembered it, and this is what he said.

"As soon as you jumped in I realized what had happened and I was scared. I wanted to run and tell Grandpa what was going on, but I was afraid to because I knew they would spank us. You stayed under for quite a while but came up gasping for air, yelling at me to help you. I remember jumping up and down in one place, and then you came up again. You really looked scared and said 'Help me, help me!' You were too far away for me to reach you, but you were closer than the first time. You then went down again for what seemed like a long time. Then I saw you, you were closer than before and close to the ladder that went in the pool, and you grabbed hold of the ladder. I was able to help you because you seemed weak, but you climbed out. You were really gasping for air, and it was a while before you could speak. Uncle Homer and Grandpa never did see what went on, and you told me not to say anything to them about it and we never did. You seemed dizzy to me."

I told Gene I didn't remember being out of breath or even being in the pool that long. I didn't remember coughing or being dizzy or anything like that. I told him I had never told anyone about that incident until right then. He couldn't believe that and wondered why not. I told him about my life passing before me. He couldn't believe that either. He told me he would have had to tell someone about it when I told him what it was like. Then I told him the reason I never told anyone about it: because I knew they wouldn't believe me. I explained to Gene how that experience changed my life forever, and that is why I read the Bible from cover to cover and the New Testament several times. I purchased the complete set of Barclay's Commentaries and studied them carefully. I realize now that humans are much more than we think we are. I have committed my life to understanding who I am and what I am doing here. So thank you, Carol, for asking Dad and Homer to take us swimming.

One more little story. When I was born, Carol was fifteen years old, and the oldest female sibling still living at home. She was getting ready to feed me some milk because I was crying and hungry. She went to get some milk out of the ice box but it had spoiled. She didn't know what she was going to do. It was late at night.

Carol woke my brother Johnny up, who was about ten years old, and told him he was going to have to go to one of our cows and milk her enough for my feeding. Johnny had never milked a cow at night and knew the cow would not like it one bit. The cow was sleeping, but he got her up and was able to get about a quart of milk and brought it to Carol. She fed me and had enough for my early morning feeding too.

Carol had turned into my mother, and I think there was always a connection between us: a special love for one another.

Now I want to tell some stories concerning my sister Georgia.

Georgia and her husband were married July 11, 1936, about five months after I was born. When I was about five years old, Georgia was babysitting me while Dad was working in the fields. She didn't want me to be alone, since all my brothers and my sister Ruth were at school. I am not sure what I was angry or mad about, but I am sure she was going to spank me, and so I ran outside.

Georgia and her husband Earl, along with their two children – Bernice was about two years old, and Gene, who was born on February 8, 1940, was just a baby – were the last people to live at the Other Place, so that is where I was. It was probably late April or early May. The weather was very nice and warm. Earl was not there. He was off working at his job, doing whatever that was.

Before I ran out of the house, I told Georgia that I was going home, which was about a half mile away, down past the graveyard. She told me I couldn't go because there wasn't anyone there. I took off running anyway across the yard to the lane and headed home. I was about half way to the cemetery when I looked behind me, and Georgia was on the road, about 200 yards behind me, carrying Gene, and Bernice was close behind her. She was yelling at me to come back, but I just kept running.

I got to the corner at the top of the hill and turned north past the graveyard and headed home. When I got to the front yard of our house, I looked back up the hill towards the graveyard. Georgia and her kids were not visible. I went into the house. Georgia was right. There was no one there. I was afraid that she might still be coming and didn't know what to do. I couldn't go back. I would get a spanking for sure.

Then I got it in my head that I would just go to the school house, which was more than another half mile north and west of our house. Our house was on top of a hill, and you could see the school house off in the distance. I went down the lane and looked back up the hill towards the graveyard. Georgia was not in sight. I turned north. I ran down the hill to the far corner, which was about a quarter of a mile. This was where Uncle Harvey, my grandma's brother, lived. I then turned west up the hill past old Bill Hightree's house. When I got to the top of the hill in front of Hightree's house, on the left, I could then see the school house on the right, still about a quarter of a mile ahead.

BILL HIGHTREE, HIS HOUSE AND DOG, CIRCA 1940

By the way, I didn't like going by Bill Hightree's house. He was a scary looking old man who always looked like he needed to take a bath. He occasionally would be walking around in his front yard right next to the road with his cane, and he would stare at me when I walked, or, I should say, ran by. I thought he must be one hundred years old. He had some goats also, and they went into that old run down house of his sometimes, and he liked to play his fiddle.

BILL HIGHTREE WITH FIDDLE

It was about this time on my journey to the school house that I thought, "What am I going to do when I get there?" It was probably two o'clock in the afternoon. I had been to the school house before, but never in the middle of the day. I knew all of my brothers and my sister Ruth were there, and I would just have to look for them. I decided after I got there not to go in the front large double doors, which were the closest, on the south side of the school house, but to go in the back door on the northeast corner of the school house, next to the outdoor basketball court. There was a well with a pump right there with a dipper, just a few steps to the east of the basketball court, and so I pumped myself a drink, since I was pretty thirsty after all that running.

I went to the door, but the door knob was pretty high and I could hardly reach it, but I finally got it to turn and opened the door. I was in the lower floor of the school house, and all of the students were upstairs. I was really getting pretty nervous and thought maybe this wasn't such a good idea, and I thought about turning around and going back home. When I think about it now, however, I realize I eventually made a brave but scary decision: I decided to go up the stairs, straight ahead, and find someone.

Then one of those miracles that always happens happened: my brother Joe Dean came walking down the stairs, probably to get a drink or to go to the outdoor toilets about a hundred yards down the hill from the well, and so I happily ran up to him. I didn't know it then, but he was a senior at that time. He said, "Lee Roy, what are you doing here?" I don't know what I told him, but it had to be a lie. I couldn't say, "I am mad at Georgia and ran away." I guess I put him in a bad spot because he had to decide what to do. He said, "You look pretty sweaty and dirty. I need to clean you up a little bit." There was a bench right by the door I had just come in with a pan on top of it and a mirror. He put some water in it from a gravity drinking fountain that was right there and washed my face and hands. He then took a comb out of his pocket, combed my hair, and took me upstairs.

I don't remember what happened right after Joe Dean took me to the classrooms, but I ended up in Wendell's. I am sure it caused some chaos, with the students wondering, "What the heck is he doing here anyway?" I sat with Wendell at his desk until school was out. The teacher gave me a pencil and a Big Chief tablet to draw on. I was happy as a Lark! The punishment I was going to get for my dastardly deed was as far away as the moon in my thought process. That part of my adventure I have blocked out of mind, and I have no idea what happened when I got home, but I bet it wasn't good.

CIVIL BEND CONSOLIDATED SCHOOL

Another story relating to my sister Georgia is about something that happened when she was twenty years old. This happened, in other words, shortly after I was born. There was a teacher in the Civil Bend Consolidated School by the name of Lovejoy, and he and his wife wanted to take me and care for me in my first months of infancy, since I had lost my mother. I never did know whether they just wanted to help Dad out for a short while until he got over the shock of losing his wife or whether they wanted to adopt me. Georgia had it in her mind they were planning on keeping me permanently, and she told me she was mad as hell.

After the Lovejoys had me for a couple of weeks with no reporting in, she went to Dad and told him, and these were her words to me when I was grown, "By God, you go over there and bring that baby home. We will raise that kid." He did. My sister Carol, who was fifteen at the time of my birth, pretty much told me a similar story when I was fifteen years old. That was before Georgia told me. If that is true, then I owe Georgia a lot for keeping me in the family that I have dearly loved. If it isn't true, then obviously Dad came and got me anyway. If it is true, then I would like to think that Dad would still have come to get me. If Dad hadn't come to get me, then I probably would have found out later in life, and I like to think I would have been a mature person and come to Dad and told him not to feel guilty, because that would have been a lot for any person to bear.

My brother Johnny told me a little story about something that happened during that period while I was being taken care of by the Lovejoys. They had two children of their own: a son who was about ten years old and a younger daughter who was about four years old. Evidently the little daughter tried to feed me some peanut butter and I might have gotten a little choked, but everything turned out all right. She got scolded, but she thought since she liked peanut butter she just wanted me to enjoy it also. Johnny told me the Lovejoys were really nice people.

Another memory I have, this time related to my sister Ruth, probably occurred when I was about six years old. We got electricity when I was five, so it was probably soon after that. Dad had purchased a Westinghouse refrigerator. I hated to see that happen because our old icebox would need a twenty-five pound block of ice pretty often. The ice truck would come by every few days, and I always liked to go out and visit with the driver. I would watch him take his pick and break down a bigger piece of ice, probably about a hundred pound chunk. The ice chips would fly. He would give me a small piece to melt in my mouth, and I really liked that a lot on hot summer days. With the arrival of that refrigerator, those days were gone forever.

That refrigerator held so much more than the old ice box, and it was right in the kitchen, which made it a lot handier to get into. We would put a full crock of whole cow's milk in the refrigerator every day or two. The crock held at least a half-gallon of milk, and overnight the cream would rise to the top. We put that in our cereal and fruit, and boy did that taste good, especially with a little sugar.

One thing I did on the sly was take a spoon, push the cream back that formed on top of the cow's milk, take a piece of homemade bread sprinkled with sugar, just sort of lay it on top of the milk, and then pull that slice of bread out and eat it. That was really good too. I would then push the cream back in place and hopefully no one would be the wiser. I was of course careful not to be caught. My sister Ruth figured it out, however, and told me to quit doing that. The way she figured it out was because the cream was always wrinkled some, and you could tell someone was up to no good. I don't think she ever told on me though, and I am pretty sure I couldn't resist and kept on doing it.

One more thing about milk. Ruth would help make two interesting things with milk that always intrigued me as a little boy: butter and cottage cheese. Milk would go sour, sometimes intentionally and sometimes not. We would take the sour milk, put it in a large sauce pan, and then heat it to 185 degrees using a candy thermometer. We'd then remove it from the heat and add three tablespoons of vinegar per gallon of milk, gently stirring until the curds and whey separated. We'd then pour everything through a colander lined with cheesecloth, rinsing everything thoroughly and squeezing the water out. We'd then tie the cheesecloth in a knot and hang it on a clothesline for three or four hours, then pour the cheese in a large bowl, and then crumble it with a large spoon to get the size we wanted. Refrigerated, the cottage cheese was always good for at least a week, and it always tasted four times better than the cottage cheese you can buy in grocery stores today.

When we made homemade butter, because we couldn't afford a butter churn, we simply put cream in a half-gallon mason jar and added a little salt. We would fill a jar about 2/3 to 3/4 full, twist on the cap, and start shaking. It took about fifteen to thirty minutes for butter to form. Sometimes the brothers would take turns shaking, and that butter was really good, and certainly better than you could ever buy in a store, probably because of the salt. The thin milk that was left was the best buttermilk ever. The buttermilk you buy in the grocery store is really too thick and not nearly as good as that buttermilk. That taste as well is gone forever.

But back to my sister Ruth!

When I was a kid, say between five and ten years old, a penny was actually a sum of money I was tickled to get my hands on. I was always searching around the house in my spare time for a penny wherever I could find one. I would even look outside the house where maybe a penny might have fallen out of someone's pocket, and you would be surprised how often I would find one. I looked upstairs where we boys slept, hoping I might find a penny on the floor. I didn't consider it stealing. I went on the premise of finders keepers.

You need to understand what a penny would buy in those days. At the General Store in Civil Bend a penny would buy a Baby Ruth or Butterfinger candy bar. A regular Baby Ruth and Butterfinger candy bar cost a nickel, but penny candy bars came in a strip, and Chrisy, the owner of the General Store, would tear off one, and those were only a penny. They were nothing to be sneezed at. They were at least as big as my index finger, which was big enough to nibble on for quite a while.

I would say that I could find a way to get a penny at least once a week. Sometimes I would ask Dad for a penny, and he might give me one if he had one in his pocket. When I would get hold of a penny I couldn't wait to spend it, and I would walk to the General Store in Civil Bend, just about a mile away.

I was well-known in Civil Bend even at that young age. Chrisy was a good friend of my Dad, as well as the friend of the Spit and Whittle Gang. They were older men often hanging around the store, and when they saw me coming they would always greet me and ask me what I was buying that day. I really didn't know their names but they knew me.

CIVIL BEND GENERAL STORE: EXTERIOR, CIRCA 1940

Once in a great while I might find a nickel or a dime. When I did, I would run in the house showing it off to my brothers. If Dad was there I would ask him if I could keep it, and he would always say finders keepers, but those times were rare. I know for sure that once in a great while Dad would give me a nickel. I guess I would catch him in a good mood. Whenever those rare moments did occur, besides jumping up and down with joy, I had some big decisions to make. My most favorite thing to buy at the General Store was a bottle of Whistle Pop: a large, ten ounce bottle of orange pop that was the best tasting stuff ever. In fact, I have an antique bottle right here in my library, which I found in an antique shop a couple of years ago, just to remind me of the joy of those memories of drinking my favorite drink of all time. Anyway, the decision I had to make was, do I want that bottle of Whistle Pop or five candy bars? Whistle Pop almost always won.

Well, what does that have to do with my sister Ruth?

One day I was searching for a penny in the house and went into Ruth's bedroom downstairs. On top of the clothes dresser was a cigar box. I opened it up, and what I found was unbelievable. It was full of money. Paper money. There were $5, $10 and $20 bills. This box belonged to Ruth. It had her name on it. I mean there was a lot of them. I thought, "How did she get all this money?" I thought, "She will never miss it if I just take one of the $5 bills." I don't think it entered my mind that I was stealing because she had so much, and that $5 would buy me a lot of candy bars and Whistle Pop. So off to the General Store I ran.

Chrisy was there with his son, Dean, who was my brother Johnny's age. Right there where you paid was one of those old antique glass counters that had some loose chocolates on display, which looked like the Russell Stover candy you would see today, and I just had to have some. I told Chrisy I wanted ten of those. He said, "Do you have some money?" I told him I did. Then he did something strange. He reached down there, got a piece, and broke it in two. He did that with ten pieces, throwing away a couple of them. He told me that would be fifteen cents. I reached up as high as I could, because I was so short, and plopped down that $5 bill. He looked at it and said to me, "Lee Roy, that isn't money." I said, "It isn't?" He said, "No, this is just a coupon."

Even at that age I knew I had made a bad mistake. I told him I was sorry, but I thought it was money. "I guess I can't pay." He looked frustrated and said, "I've broken the candy, so I will just give it to you." He gave me the coupon back. I was feeling so guilty, I don't think I even thanked him for the candy. I took the coupon back home and put it back in the cigar box and never told anybody about it.

When I got older I would think about that experience, and I was sure Chrisy must have told Dad about that. Dad, however, never mentioned it to me, and if he knew about it, then why didn't I get a spanking for that? When I get to heaven I hope I can talk to Chrisy and Dad about that and tell them both I am sorry and that I asked God to forgive me. As I got older I realized why Chrisy broke all that candy. I am sure he was checking it for worms! I can find all that out up there.

When I was a grown man I told Ruth about it and she laughed, telling me she never did get enough of those coupons to mail them off for a blouse. She told me those coupons were in the Sunday paper for a long time, and she kept cutting them out, but she needed $500 worth, they quit putting them in the paper, and she couldn't collect enough.

When I was a little older, probably in the fifth or sixth grade, I would have been ten to twelve years old, and I always called Ruth "Ruthie." It was about this time of my life that I started getting interested in girls. Seems like I always had a crush on a girl at school that I would play hide and seek or some other game with, where I could hold her hand or sneak a kiss. Before long they would find someone else to be their boyfriend, so I would find someone else to be my girlfriend. This happened probably every six months or so.

At this particular time I had a crush on a girl named Ruby. Of course, my brothers heard about it and would tease me about her and say things like, "Did you kiss Ruby today?" Ruby lived about a mile from us, and they might say something like, "Are you going to walk up to Ruby's today and play house with her?" Just stuff like that to get me upset.

I was home one day, and a bunch of my brothers and Ruthie were passing time away. I was in the living room with my brothers and Ruth was in the kitchen. I was daydreaming about Ruby. I was talking with my brothers about a card game that Ruth was teaching me how to play, and they wanted to know what the game was called. I yelled into the kitchen and said, "Ruby, what's the name of that card game you are teaching me?" One of my brothers said, "What did you say! Hey guys did you hear what Lee Roy just said?" I knew I was caught, but, before you could blink your eyes, I came up brilliantly with this "Ruthie, what's the name of that card game you are teaching me?" It worked to perfection. The brother who thought he had caught me said, "Oh, I thought you said Ruby." I was so proud of myself. Ruth laughed and told them the name of the game. It was called "Touring." She didn't say anything, but I think she knew exactly what I said!

Now I'd like to tell you some stories related to my oldest sister, Myrtle.

I asked Myrtle about what it was like growing up on the farm when she was little. Here are some of her answers.

"The girls would wash and dry dishes. For the little ones we would put a dishpan on a chair because they weren't tall enough. Mom used to tell me I was going to be a good housekeeper someday. There was a lot of housework to do: snapping beans, hauling peas, stemming gooseberries, making beds, mopping floors, preparing meals, and stuff like that."

"Sunday was church day. We rode a two seated buggy, or a horse pulling a wagon, when I was little. We got a car later. Mom only missed church when she or someone was sick. She was pregnant a lot. She made chicken and dumplings a lot, and she was a really good cook. We baked bread almost every other day. Monday was wash day. We used a washboard. We got a washing machine when I was little. I really did like that washing machine, and Mom did too. Lowell got his sleeve caught in the wringer and broke his arm when he was ten years old. That was the only broken bone any of the children ever got that I know of. I always thought that it was a miracle given the way the boys got thrown off the mules and horses, jumping out of haylofts and falling out of trees, etcetera. We used old grease from the frying pan mixed with lye to make soap, and we used a little bluing in the rinse water to make the white clothes whiter."

"I went to Powell School my first four years. There were two grocery stores in Civil Bend, a Central office, and Dr. Hardinger's office. That was the same doctor who delivered you when you were born at our Home Place in 1936. My school lunch was usually a fried egg sandwich, dried vegetables, and fruits. That was before canning became popular. We soaked hard field corn in lye water to make both yellow and white hominy. We had a smokehouse to cure bacon and ham. The smokehouse burned down when I was in high school. We lost all our ham and bacon. Dad was below the barn when the fire occurred."

"My favorite subject in high school was math. My least favorite was science. I liked sports a lot, and I traveled to Jameson, Pattonsburg, and Gallatin to play basketball. Mildred Shaw was in my class, but I did not like her much. She was a teacher's pet because her Aunt, Esther Crank, was a good friend of hers, and Mrs. Crank was the Superintendent of the school. Mildred was not very good at sewing, but she beat me for valedictorian anyway.

"Mary Ann Cornett was my best friend, and she stayed all night at our house a couple of times. We went on double dates together. Uncle Virgil gave me my first 'store bought' dress. Mom made all our clothes. She would look at a pattern in the Wards catalog. She was a really good seamstress. She would make dresses from sacks with different pretty patterns on them. She would get these sacks from the dry goods store when they purchased flour, sugar and other stuff in bulk, even feed from the grain elevator for the hogs and chickens. That was very common back then. My friends were jealous because Mom made the best dresses in Civil Bend."

"Virgil Huffman was my boyfriend. He rode his horse to pick me up with his buggy. One day it rained some and the road became muddy. He had me ride in the buggy while he walked his horse. I thought that was very considerate."

"The most influential person in my life was my Mom, but the most influential person next to my mother was Bessy June Brown, who I met in Cameron, Missouri when I was in school there a short time after graduating from high school. I stayed there in their house and worked for them. Her husband was a dentist, and I was their maid and housekeeper. Mrs. Brown was really good to me. After attending for a year, they closed that school down. I wanted to become a teacher, but Mrs. Brown told me to go to Kansas City Central Business College and become a secretary. I worked as a waitress while attending college there, and the largest tip I ever got was twenty-five cents."

"Dad was a hard worker and well-behaved. He got up early and worked farmland on the Grand River bottom. He had cows to milk when he got home."

"I remember Dad chewing Olen and Lowell out for going to the river when it was out of its banks. Georgia caught her dress on fire once because the damper on the stove was open. Mother burned her hand really bad when I was four years old. She had her hand wrapped in cloth for quite a while. We used castor oil for everything. Homer almost fell in a well one time, but Dad rescued him because a nail in a board caught him. He was four years old. Olen ran off once with his little red wagon. When he was older he wanted to quit school. Dad said okay, I need some help to cut wood for the cook stove. Olen said he would go back to school."

Myrtle was the oldest of all the siblings, and I was the youngest. She was born in 1911, and I was born in 1936. Twenty-five years was the difference in our ages. When I was young, I didn't see Myrtle very much. She left home when she graduated from high school and was out in the world doing her thing. She did come home some, but the one thing I remember about her even back then was that she was a really good cook. She made some of the best pies I ever ate, and even to this day I prefer pies over cakes because of her.

During World War II, her husband Stanley Redd was serving his time while she and her daughter Sharon, another one of my many nieces, lived on the farm with us. This was probably around 1944 –1945. I would have been eight to ten years old. Sharon would have been one to two years old, so I had a couple of years of Myrtle's good cooking. I know she helped with the canning a lot then too.

As a young boy I was really ignorant about the birds and the bees and everything else. I believed in the Easter Bunny and Santa Claus until I was ten years old. I really didn't quite understand why Myrtle was staying with us at that time. Stanley would come home on furlough every now and then, but I knew he wasn't fighting in the war like my brothers Miles and Lowell. When Stanley would come home he would bring home lots of Snickers candy bars, and Myrtle would share one every now and then with us younger kids.

I noticed one day that Myrtle was getting fat and was sick a lot, and I asked Dad what was the matter with her and why she was gagging and throwing up all the time. He said she was pregnant and was going to have a baby. I had no idea. The twins, Joe and Jerry, were born a short while after that.

I had a lot of growing up to do when I left home at seventeen years of age, after graduating from high school. I learned there was a lot I didn't know about life. I remember when I was nineteen and in college, I was in lab making a medicine called N.F. Antiseptic Solution. After we had made it, we had to write up a report on its uses, so I looked that up. One of the uses was as a douche. Most of my colleagues were quite a bit older than me because they were going on the G.I. Bill and had served in the military, so their college was paid for. I asked my lab partner, who was probably twenty-five, what a douche was. He laughed and told every person in class what I had asked. That was only one of many times I embarrassed myself because of my naivety.

Myrtle was very kind to me my first year of college in 1953. She let me stay at her and Stanley's house. I slept in the basement that year, and she fed me one meal a day with her family. Stanley even invited me to their Friday night out at his favorite restaurant. It didn't cost me a dime. I would babysit with the kids once in a while. I enjoyed that and got to know the kids pretty well. They have grown up to be good and decent people.

Myrtle lived to be 103. Sharon, living close by with her husband Charles Usher, took care of her wonderfully. Joe and Jerry became doctors and lived in California, but they did come home regularly.

CIVIL BEND SCHOOL HISTORY

During the early days in the area around which I was born, probably from 1840 to 1870, a simple log cabin provided for one's education. About 1870, however, the log cabin facility was discontinued, and children started attending various rural schools in the district. There were four such schools. There was the Union School and the Conover School. There was also the Lee School, which obtained its name because it was near the Taylor Lee farm, though it was sometimes called the Center School because of its location in the district. Then there was the Oak Grove School, sometimes called the Powell School, and it was located just south of the Civil Bend Christian Church. This was the school my Dad, Russell Bruner, attended. My sister Myrtle attended this same school her first four years, and Olen as well for a year or two.

A picture exists from the *Pattonsburg Call* that shows my Dad in a class picture from his old schoolhouse, taken in 1904, in the second row, eighth from the left, right above the Oak Grove School chalk board sign. Two of his brothers, Virgil and Paul, are also in the picture. Virgil is the fellow with the dapper hat just to the left of the tall guy on the back row, and Paul is in the front row holding the sign, right in front of Dad. These schools remained the education facilities until 1921, when the various local schools were consolidated.

POWELL SCHOOL, CIVIL BEND, 1904

Even earlier in its history, the Civil Bend area was within hollering distance of many of the infamous Jesse James outlaw gang's bank and train robberies. Here is one of the lesser known stories of one of their robberies and gun-fights.

The 1869 bank robbery at Gallatin, the 1881 train robbery at Winston, and the 1883 trial of Frank James in Gallatin aren't the only significant incidences involving the James Gang in Daviess County, Missouri. In 1871, a posse chased the outlaws following a bank robbery in Corydon, Iowa, exchanging gunfire at one of the Civil Bend schools.

About 1:00 p.m. on Saturday, June 3, 1871, the Ocobock Brother's Bank in Corydon was robbed by four men of $5,244.07 in currency and stamps. The vault and money drawer were completely emptied. Ted Wock, the only em-ployee in the bank, looked up the barrel of a large Colt revolver, which he described as being loaded, with a barrel eight to ten inches long. It was held by a thick-set, well-built, but not very tall, sunburned man. Another man filled a saddlebag with the money.

As many as ninety men followed the gang south to the Missouri line. Some took each of the trails heading south to Trenton and Princeton, Missouri, and some went east to the railroad at Allerton, located right at the Iowa and Mis-souri state line. The C&SW Railroad, then under construction, would not be completed to Cameron until late in September.

Most good James Gang books state that the gang consisted of Jesse (Blinky Dingus) James, Frank James, Cole Younger, and Clell (Hines) Miller. Miller was later arrested at Cameron in 1872 and acquitted of the Corydon robbery, apparently because there was reasonable doubt as to his participation.

Anyway, one small group of the posse followed the trail to Leon, Iowa, on Saturday, then to Pleasant Plains and Eagleville, Missouri, on Sunday. They followed the robbers until noon, when a gunfight broke out at Civil Bend Center School, or Lee School. The posse in pursuit was led by Iowa farmer John A. Corbit. He was followed by Corydon officer Charles R. Wright, hotel owner James D. Coddington, and two Missourians. Coddington was later able to identify two of the robbers who had stayed at his hotel in Corydon on Fri-day night, and he identified Miller as one of the men in the gang seen near Civil Bend. The fight, as reported in the papers, took place on June 5, 1871, at the Civil Bend School No. 4 and the school's stable.

The posse came from the north and saw the gang of four men sitting, resting with their backs against the school building. Money wrappers were left at this spot, so the gang may have been dividing the loot in order to split up. The gang jumped up and ran for the stable, where they had left their guns and horses. Farmer Corbit later testified that the day was cloudy and rainy. He said that the school house was four or five rods west of the north-south road where the stable stood, or about 180 steps southwest of the school. Officer Wright went with Coddington to the west of the stable in a wheat field.

They got within sixty yards of the stable, with Corbit about 120 steps to the east of the stable on the road, when the gang, cornered, started shooting. Coddington called for a surrender, but one lone voice called from the stable, "We cannot see it." After about twenty gunshots were exchanged, the gang mounted their horses in the stable and fled south. At least one shot took effect, killing a posse man's horse. Found at the school house stable was a linen coat, a pair of gloves, four or five large size revolver holsters, and a large revolver with "W and W" on the butt.

The posse once again caught the gang about two and one-half miles south at the farm of Freeland Boyer, near Cottonwood Creek. There, however, an accidental early shot fired by a posse member resulted in another escape before the rest were in a position to prevent it. The gang had fresh horses, and the posse turned back. Clell Miller was later killed by Henry Wheeler on September 7, 1876 during a robbery in Northfield, Minnesota. Miller was only twenty -six, experiencing twelve years of high adventure as an outlaw.

Jim Snider, of Pattonsburg, provides a twist on this research from the story told to him by his father and Freeland Boyer, who lived until 1915. Mr. Snider relates that after the gunfight at the school house, the James Gang stopped at Freeland Boyer's well to get water for their horses. When the Iowa posse got there, the gang decided to fight it out. Not surprisingly, the posse members told a different story about their loss of interest in overtaking the gang after a long chase. More information on all this can be found at the Daviess County Historical Society.

Whatever the early crime dramas of the region, residents began to see the need for a consolidated school system, and several times elections were held for this need, but the propositions were always voted down. Finally, however, on April 23, 1921, the patrons of the Powell, Lee, Union, and Conover Schools succeeded in gaining the majority of votes. The trouble now confronting them was securing a site for the consolidated building. The elected members of the first Board of Education set out to solve this problem, and the dilemma was soon answered by Dr. S.L. Hardinger, who offered some of his vacant buildings for the purpose, and the same were gladly accepted. Miss Claire Hardinger was elected Superintendent, with Miss Claire Bell and Miss Ethel Giseburt appointed as grade teachers.

Three months before the second term of school these buildings were still not ready to be occupied. A mass meeting was therefore held, and a Building Association was formed. Shares amounting to $3,000 were sold, and plans for constructing a school building were made. A ten year lease on land belonging to A. Canfield was obtained, and work on the building was begun. Much of the work was done by donation, and the structure was ready for occupancy by the opening of school, just six weeks after it was started.

In 1925, the Civil Bend consolidated school was placed on the list of first class high schools in the state, and it retained that status until it closed in 1948. In 1932, the lease on the school grounds expired and the district purchased the land. A few years afterwards the shares were bought in and the school now belonged to the district.

The Parent Teachers Association was a very important organization for the new Civil Bend school, providing many otherwise unavailable conveniences. The directors at that time were Andrew Carnagey, President, along with Clyde Young, Clyde Frost, Walter Frost, Dwight Hibbs, and Russell Bruner, who would become my Dad eleven years later, Secretary and Treasurer. Dad remained a part of that school board for twenty consecutive years.

Miss Foley was my first grade teacher in 1941. I was just barely five years old. I remember her quite well, however, and have always given her much credit for getting me off to a good start at such a young age. I really liked her and have a lot of good memories of that year. She left after my first year, but she was there a while because she was a teacher as early as 1932.

One day in Miss Foley's class we were having a spelling test, and I remember one of the words was "does." Mr. Yancey, the Superintendent, had come in to visit our room for a while, and he squeezed into my little desk seat and was watching me spell. I spelled the word "dose" and looked up at him, but he was frowning. I took my eraser and erased the "se" and changed it to "es," looked up at him again, and he had a big smile on his face! I was ready for the next word. I didn't know it at the time, but he was a good friend of my Dad's. When I think of that moment now, I wonder if my Dad had asked him to come in and check to see how I was doing because I was so young.

I received my first seven years of education at the Civil Bend consolidated school: one building with all twelve grades for all the children in the area. The average class size was probably about four students. Grades one through four were in one room with one teacher. Grades five through eight were also in one room with one teacher, and grades nine through twelve were basically in one room with two or three teachers. There was a music room but no band. There was some singing, and there was a stage for some small plays and performances. There was a typing room and one room in the lower level for some special high school classes. There was a large coal furnace on the lower level. There was a small room where meals were prepared some years. My nephew, Gene Bridgman, said his mother, my sister Georgia, prepared some of those meals. I remember mainly taking our own lunch to school in a paper sack or wrapped up in a newspaper with a rubber band holding it together. Maybe a ham and cheese, egg salad, or peanut butter and jelly sandwich and maybe some fresh fruit such as a banana, grapes, or an apple.

There was a small dressing room to dress up for sports. The basketball court was outside, and we played on dirt. In the basement were ping pong tables. The boys and girls toilets were outside about a hundred yards down the hill from the school building. There was no plumbing or running water. Water was outside by the basketball court where the well was situated, though inside there was a small water fountain, gravity fed.

When playing basketball it was very dusty and dirty. There were no showers to clean up after recess. When it was windy the dust blew in your eyes. There was a place inside by the fountain where you could wash your hands and face on a community towel. The floors throughout the building were wooden and always greasy. If you fell down or scooted on the floor while playing marbles inside it was hard not to get your clothes dirty. With the coal furnace, that was a natural situation after many years.

There was a big bell outside the building, but I think it only rang when school started. There was a small Superintendent's office that housed a trophy case. There may have been a dozen or so trophies. There was also a large paddle with three holes on the wall for spanking when you misbehaved. I was told the holes were in the paddle to make the spanking hurt worse. I think it was there to scare you more than anything else. I don't remember anyone getting a spanking, but my older brothers and sisters did remember such occasions.

I was a smart and good student, and I believe that all of the Bruners were. I don't think any of us got into very much trouble, though I think some of my older brothers were a little more ornery at times.

I never went to high school in Civil Bend, but all my brother and sisters did except Gayle. He, like me, went all four years of high school in Pattonsburg, and Roger went to Pattonsburg his Junior and Senior years.

When Civil Bend competed in basketball, most of the other towns also had outside courts. The average score of games played back then was probably something like 12 to 8. Of course, I played basketball inside the gym in Pattonsburg, so I was lucky. Going to school in Civil Bend was quite an experience, not anything like school today.

LIFE EXPERIENCES

I liked to read when I was a kid, starting about seven or eight years old. Not so much books but magazines, comic books, and anything that looked interesting. Dad subscribed to the *St. Joseph Gazette*, a newspaper printed and distributed in St. Joseph, Missouri. It was a daily paper that was thrown in our yard every morning, but on Sunday it was special. In daily issues the comic strips would just be a sequence of four pictures in black and white, but on Sundays there would be twelve or sixteen pictures in color of my favorite comic strips. Dick Tracy was my favorite, with all those villains, including Flattop, Prune Face, The Mole, Gravel Gertie, the Brow, B.O. Plenty, Mumbles, and many others. There were good guys like Junior, Tess Trueheart, and Sam Catchem. The two-way wrist radio was cool too.

I liked Gasoline Alley and Li'l Abner, with his voluptuous girlfriend Daisy Mae Scragg, and the bad luck character Joe Btfsplk, who always had a cloud over his head, plus Mammy and Pappy Yokum. They all lived in Dogpatch, a hillbilly paradise, just like me.

There were so many excellent cartoons, such as Alley Oop, Mutt and Jeff, Little Orphan Annie, Dagwood, and Blondie. They'll do it every time. Don Winslow of the Navy, Felix the Cat, Flash Gordon, Batman, Fearless Fosdick, Pogo, Sad Sack, Gene Autry, Grin and Bear It, Joe Palooka, Bringing up Father with Maggie and Jiggs, Popeye, Ripley's Believe It or Not, Superman, and scads of others.

There was a lot of other stuff in the newspaper. Dad loved the St. Louis Cardinals, and he and I both could not wait to get yesterday's scores if we hadn't listened to them on the radio the day before. We wanted to see who pitched, and, in 1941, see how that new rookie Stan Musial did. He was the greatest player of the St. Louis Cardinals in history, in my opinion, and probably the greatest man to ever play the game.

The mailman, as you already know, was another important person in my life. I always got the mail every day. He came by almost every day no matter the weather. He came about 11:00 a.m., and I would run down to the mailbox and get our mail as soon as he stopped. I very seldom got any personal mail, but I did write an occasional letter to one of my brothers and they would normally write me back. I remember watching my sister Ruth writing a letter to someone in the family one time, and I asked her if I could watch. Here is how it started. "Dear Olen, I hope you can read this letter because I am writing it on my lap and it may not be as easy to read." I thought that was a really good way to start a letter, so I got my Big Chief tablet and went to the dining room table and decided to write a letter to my brother Joe Dean. Here is how it started. "Dear Joe Dean, I hope you can read this letter okay because I am writing it on my lap." After that, though, I just wrote about what I was doing in school, noting that I knew how to spell. I would bother Ruth and ask her how to spell certain words that I wasn't sure about. I couldn't write cursive yet, but my printing was not too bad. Ruth showed me how to address the envelope and I did that by myself. I put a three cent stamp on it and mailed it.

The very next day I went to the mailbox looking for an answer from Joe Dean. I went every day for a week or so and by golly I did get a letter from him, and I couldn't wait to open it. He had printed it so I could read it. There were some words I didn't know, and Ruth helped me with those words. I really didn't care too much what it said, though, because he had sent me a dollar bill and that was all I could think about. He had sent it to me for my birthday, and Dad gave me a nickel a week to go to the General Store. I wasn't very sharp or I would have written all my older brothers and sisters telling them they could send me a dollar for my birthday if they wanted to, even though my birthday was already past. I guess I wasn't raised to think that way.

There is something extra special we got in the mail. Every April my Dad would order baby chicks from somewhere, and believe it or not they would come through the mail. When I tell this story to people their jaw drops in disbelief, but it is true. The mailman would bring them up the lane and hand deliver them. They came in a box about four feet on each side and about six inches high. The boxes had holes about the size you could put a small marble through on all four sides, and there might have been some on top too, as that way the baby chickens could get plenty of air and not smother. I think there was twenty-five or fifty chicks in each box, and there was probably one hundred chicks in all. There unfortunately was always two or three that didn't survive.

Dad would take these baby chickens out and put them in our brooder house, and there was a large metal tent-like thing in the middle with a light on the inside at the top to keep them warm. They were so cute, and we kept them in that house until they got big enough to let outside. We raised them to eat when they got big enough, and we had a lot of fried chicken. When they got pretty good-sized we would take a day and slaughter them, pick off the feathers, and then take the meat to the locker plant in Pattonsburg. One or two years we grew a whole lot of them for my brother Homer to serve in his restaurant in St. Joseph.

When I was a small boy I remember being sick a lot, always coughing and having sore throats. We rarely went to the doctor as far as I can remember. When I was five years old my Dad told me he was going to come to school and pick me up and we were going to the doctor. It was in the morning about half way to lunch time when he picked me up. I don't remember being any more sick than usual, and I don't remember being nervous about going to the doctor.

While we were driving to the doctor it seemed to me to be taking quite a while, and so I asked my Dad why we were going to the doctor and where were we going? He said that I was going to have my tonsils taken out so I would not be coughing and sick so much. That seemed like a good idea to me. He said we were going to a doctor in Bethany, which was about thirty miles from our house, and we would be there before too much longer.

When we got there it was a large house, and they took me straight to a table so large that I had to have a chair to get up to it. The doctor told me he was going to let me go to sleep, but I told him I wasn't sleepy. He told me not to worry because he was going to put something over my nose and mouth that would make me sleepy, and then I would go to sleep for a little while, and when I woke up my tonsils would be gone and I wouldn't be sick and cough as much anymore. He asked me if I could count to ten and I told him I could. Then he asked me if I could count backwards from ten to one. I told him I had never done that before but I was pretty sure I could. He put a mask over my nose and told me to breathe in and start counting backwards starting with ten. But before you start I want you to know when you wake up your throat is going to be very sore for a while. I didn't like that idea very much, but I said ok. I started counting 10-9-8-7~6~5 and fell asleep.

They were giving me chloroform, but I didn't know that, and when I woke up I was in a normal bed and was really groggy. Then all of a sudden I realized that my throat was really sore. It was sorer than I ever remembered, and I needed to throw-up. I threw-up in a big white pan. It was really bloody and it scared me, but the doctor said not to worry, that it was a good thing for me to throw-up, that I wouldn't throw-up anymore, that my Dad could take me home pretty soon, and that I would feel better when I got home in my own bed.

About an hour later my Dad drove me home, but I could hardly swallow. My throat was really sore all the way home, and I could not wait to get home in my own bed so my throat wouldn't hurt anymore. My sister Ruth had stayed home from school and fixed me a bed on the couch in the parlor, and I could tell that she was trying to make it not hurt. She told me she would get me anything I wanted. I told her the doctor said I could sip on some warm lemonade when I got home and that would help my sore throat. He said since I liked soft-boiled eggs I could have one of those if I got hungry, so she fixed me one of those, and it did feel better going down my throat, but it was still hard to swallow. I asked Ruthie, which is what I called her, how long my throat was going to hurt like this, and she said it would probably feel better in the morning.

Ruthie asked me if I would like to read the comic strips in the paper that had come that morning. I normally got the paper every morning. When I went to school I would go get the paper and bring it to the house, but I wouldn't have time to read it until after school was out. I always read the comic strips and, as you know, my favorite was Dick Tracy. I would immediately read the sports page and see how the Cardinals did the day before.

I slept quite a bit that day but had a hard time sleeping that night. In the morning my throat was still really sore and I was pretty mad because I didn't know it was going to hurt that much just to get my tonsils out. Ruth sympathized with me and said she felt sorry for me, but I would not be nearly as sick anymore once I got healed and would be glad. She said to just be brave.

I played cards a lot that day and didn't have to do any chores at all, and I thought that was a good deal. Ruthie was really good to me, and on the third morning I felt a lot better. Dad told me I could go back to school the next Monday, and I was happy about that. On Sunday I didn't go to church with everyone because I was still in bed, except to go outside to the bathroom. The Sunday paper was thrown in our front yard early that morning and I really liked that. All in all it wasn't such a bad deal to be pampered all that time, and I was given permission to have as many suckers as I wanted as long as I promised not to chew on them.

On Monday morning I walked to school with one of my older brothers and the teacher, Miss Foley, was really nice to me too. It wouldn't be worth it to have to do it all over again, however. You know, though, I wasn't really ever as sick as I used to be after that, so maybe it was worth it.

In general, particularly in the United States, children don't have the sicknesses they used to have. The discovery of vaccines and medicines give today's children such a huge advantage compared to when I was growing up in the 1940s. For example, when I was about eight or nine years old I got very sick with the mumps. I got them on both sides of my neck and was really miserable. It brought back memories of when I had my tonsils removed. Having the mumps was much worse, however, because of the length of time it took to heal and recover. I had trouble swallowing for several days, and my sickness lasted for about seven days.

I got the mumps in the summertime, so I didn't miss any school, but the temperature inside the house made me much more uncomfortable. We didn't know anything about air conditioning back then, and I don't remember anyone having any kind of air conditioning. I believe I read in a book or magazine when I got much older that by 1965 only ten percent of residential homes had air conditioning. Before that, it was more prevalent in the work place. I think we may have had electric fans after we got electricity in our home in 1941. My sister Ruthie was home once again, taking care of me as best as she could and making me soft-boiled eggs and toast, even though all food was hard to swallow. Of course I had the sports page and the comic strips, and thankfully the heroes and the villains just kept coming.

I was kept pretty isolated because mumps is very contagious. I don't remember if anyone else caught the mumps from me or me from them, but Gayle told me he had the mumps, and several of my brothers may have had them at the same time, but I don't think so. Gayle couldn't remember how old he was when he had them. For all of you who may be reading this story, I will tell you that mumps is a viral infection of the salivary gland. You probably will never get the mumps because you were vaccinated when you were little and probably don't even remember it.

I also had whooping cough when I was very young, probably around three years old. My sister Georgia told me that I had the disease, but of course I don't remember that. She said I was pretty sick though. I don't think I ever had chicken pox, which is a little like the measles but not nearly as bad, but you still have blisters and a rash that is short-lived. I had pink eye, or conjunctivitis, when I was about twelve or thirteen years old. I woke up one morning and couldn't open my eyes, as puss had formed and hardened a little bit. It scared me, but they washed my eyes with warm water. I was okay. My eyes stayed mattered for a couple of days and then the puss went away. I would wash my eyes several times a day with salt water. Actually, it is a pretty common infection.

But I want to tell you about maybe the worst infection I ever had as a child. That was the measles. Measles starts with a high temperature and sore eyes (conjunctivitis) and a runny nose. This lasts for a day or so, then you get small white spots inside the mouth and a very sore throat. Then you get a harsh dry cough. You get very tired, and severe aches and pains occur. You sometimes lose your appetite. It is a viral infection that is very contagious. Diarrhea and vomiting is normal. When you become exposed you normally have a ten to fourteen day waiting period as the measles incubate, and you have no signs of measles during this time. The rash consists of small red spots, some of which are slightly raised. Spots and bumps in tight clusters give the skin a splotchy appearance. The face breaks out first, particularly behind the ears and along the hairline. Over the next few days it spreads down the arms and chest, lower thighs, and feet. You become infectious to others for about eight days, four days before the rash appears and four days after. Measles become very itchy when they start to dry up, and it is hard not to scratch them.

I was isolated upstairs in bed for over a week. I was really sick. Again I read the newspaper with the comic strips and the sports page. We had a radio by then, and they let me have it. I could listen to the Cardinals on the radio almost every day or night, and that helped pass the time away.

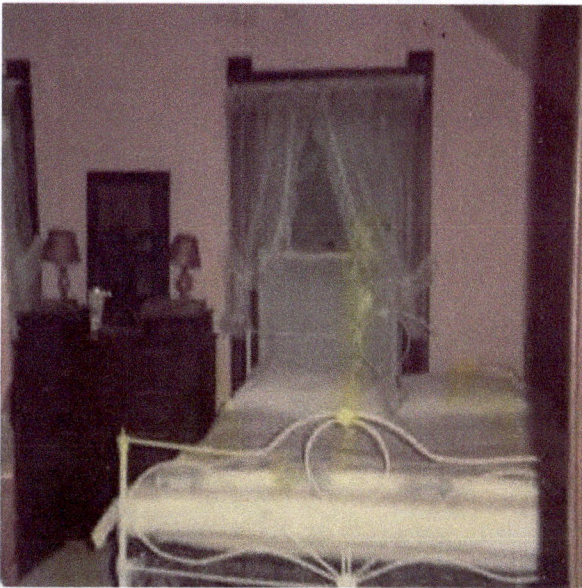

MY BEDROOM UPSTAIRS IN THE HOME PLACE

I always liked to read the Saturday Evening Post and comic books and other magazines. I slept most of the time, day and night, if I could. It got pretty lonely upstairs by myself, but except for a couple of days I would eat my three meals a day. Children today should never have measles because of the vaccines that are available, and you are very lucky you don't have to go through the pains and discomforts of these diseases.

I was not always a good little boy, as you know. I remember when I was in the third or fourth grade taking a book home from school to read. I have always enjoyed reading, and to this day, as an elderly man, I still read many books. I am pretty sure this book was for fun reading, not some book to study. On the way home after school I was goofing around with Clinton Whetstone, a class-mate of mine. I think we were throwing some gravel off the road just to see who could throw the farthest. I put the book down in a ditch beside the road, the gravel-throwing distraction made me forget to pick up the book, and I went home without it.

I thought about the book as I was getting ready for bed, thinking I would read a chapter or two, then realizing I had left it in the ditch while playing with Clinton. It was too late and too dark to go get it, and so I decided to pick it up in the morning on the way to school, bring it back home after school, and start reading it then.

I got up the next morning and, much to my chagrin, it had rained all night. I found the book right where I had left it, but it was thoroughly soaked, and water was still running in the ditch and dripping out of that book. The cover was all wrinkled. I didn't know what to do, so I decided to sneak it back into the library and return it to the shelf where I had gotten it, thinking no one would be the wiser.

Well, that afternoon, Mrs. McClung, my teacher, sternly said "Attention eve-ryone!" When she got all of our attention, she opened the library doors and I knew the jig was up. There was the book, still wet, and the shelf was even wet. She said, "Does anyone know how this wet book got on the shelf?" What could I do but admit that I did it?

I can't remember what the consequences were, but I sure did feel like a fool. I think since I admitted to the dastardly deed there wasn't too much of a pun-ishment. Probably there was no recess for a couple of days, and I think she made me take it home and show my Dad, telling me to give an oral report on the book to the class. Dad was on the school board and maybe he had to pay for the book, who knows? I may have gotten a whipping for that, but I have a tendency to forget those sorts of things.

I have a story concerning my brother Gayle that I must share.

I have mentioned a couple of times in our lives when our personalities collid-ed, especially when we were young; however, it has been written, "When I was a child I spoke as a child. I understood as a child. I thought as a child. But when I became a man I put away childish things."

This is the story, as told to me by Gayle. He said, "I was a senior in high school. You were a sophomore. We both played on the first team but played sparingly. We were the number one and number two substitutes on the team. We were playing Gallatin at Gallatin."

"Gallatin, you remember, was a much larger school, and we just could not catch them. I think we were behind a few points the whole game. In the middle of the fourth quarter we were trailing by six points, and the coach told you, Lee Roy, to go into the game. He said, 'I want you to get open, if you can, and shoot the ball and get us back into this game!' So you go, get the ball, get an open shot, and make the shot. Now we trailed by only four points. They missed their next shot. You got the ball, got another open shot, and made that shot! Now we trailed by only two points. They missed again. You took the next shot but missed, and coach called time out and took you out of the game."

"The team played back and forth, and we had gotten to within one point. With the last two minutes to go one of the starters fouled out, and the coach put me in the game. That was the game that ended with Nick Savage attempting a long shot that I rebounded and made the shot that you, Lee, thought tied the game but actually won the game, and you came running toward me on the court, putting your arms around me in celebration."

Gayle told me that the memory of us hugging one another in celebration was one of the happiest moments of his life, and when I think of that moment now I realize how we evolved, growing to love one another as we do to this day. We no longer thought as children but put away our childish things, a true characteristic we developed as Bruners growing up in Civil Bend.

Another important life experience occurred the following year, when I was a junior at Pattonsburg High School taking a biology class. My teacher was Mr. Minter. He used to teach at Civil Bend years ago and was Superintendent there. It was the first class of the day.

I and my buddy Charlie Blankenship were coming out of Home Room, because the first thing we did every day was go there to take roll and then go to our first class. We had to go through the gymnasium to go up the stairs. Lo and behold, right in the middle of the center of the court of the gym floor was a basketball. I told Charlie I was going to get that ball and take a long corner shot.

No one was allowed on the clean and shiny court with normal shoes on, so I sat down on one of the lower bleacher seats, took my shoes off, and went out on the floor to get the ball, all while Charlie patiently waited.

I came back, put the ball by my side to put my shoes back on, when suddenly Charlie stole the ball, went down to the corner of the court, shot a long shot, and made it! Well, I didn't have time to go get the ball again, so I was mad as a hornet when we went upstairs to biology class. Charlie was laughing, but I told him I would get even before the day was over.

Charlie wore long sleeved white shirts a lot, and no other student did, so I figured I would just sneak up on him from behind and do something before the day was over.

When we got to class Mr. Minter said, "Since it is such a nice day, put all of your books or whatever you brought to class and put them in your locker. We are going outside on a field trip. Meet me in the gym in five minutes." We all assembled there, and then he led us outside.

After about five minutes of walking I looked for Charlie, ready for my revenge, and saw him ahead of me with his long sleeved white shirt. I don't quite know what overcame me, but I went running quickly toward him, he did not see me, and I bit him on his back! I got a pretty good chomp too, and he said "Ouch!" real loud.

He turned around, and I was laughing really hard, and it was Mr. Minter!

I was stunned, and so was he. He didn't say a word, and I didn't either. I wanted to say what should have been a simple thing to say, "Gosh, I feel terrible Mr. Minter, I thought you were Charlie," but somehow, for some reason, I thought that would be wrong, or weird, and so I said nothing. Ever.

What a miserable field trip that was.

Most of the class was wondering what just happened, except for Charlie, who was laughing at first, but then he realized I might be in for some serious trouble.

Science was always my favorite subject in high school, and I always got "E" grades for excellent. When my grade cards came out that term, however, I had an "M", or the equivalent of today's C, and it was the only "M" I ever got in high school. When I took my grade card home, Dad understandably wanted to know what happened in biology. I told him a lie, still not knowing why I couldn't tell Mr. Minter the truth, and said I didn't know. He rightly said there was no excuse for getting an "M".

Mr. Minter and I never got along after that. I mean we hardly ever talked. I should have told him why I mistakenly bit him on the back but never did, and by the time I finally tried it was simply too late.

Let's move forward to my senior year. Mr. Minter was no longer a teacher at the school. I also had an academic rival all my years at Pattonsburg High School, and so I always wanted to know what my grades were. At the end of the year my rival was very happy to be the first to tell me I was the Salutatorian and she the Valedictorian. I asked her how she found that out, and she said she went to the Superintendent's office and asked. She said it was really close, noting there was less than a 1% difference in our grades. I congratulated her.

"You know," she said, "it was the grade in biology last year that made the difference. You made an M and I made an E-."

So that bite ended up biting me back, even though my years in high school were otherwise terrific.

As a young man, one day when I had returned home, Dad told me Mr. Minter was very sick in St. Joseph, if I wanted to see him. I thought I should, and I thought I would finally tell him about our incident many years ago, letting him know the truth. When his wife answered the door to their home, I told her who I was and that I hoped to say hello to her husband, and that I had something important I wanted to tell him. She said he was very sick but would tell him I was there.

She came back and said he would see me, but she was not sure at all if her husband would remember me. Well, she was right. He could hardly speak, I knew he was weak, and I couldn't find a way to explain one bit about the incident.

I made a bad choice many years ago, for reasons I may never understand, by not explaining truthful things when I had the chance, then I lied on top of that, then I could do nothing to make amends.

I suppose this is something that happens for one reason or another to all of us from time to time, sad to say, even when raised to know right from wrong.

SEEKING JUSTICE

I once hid from my Dad all day in a hot combine bin in the middle of the summer to avoid a whipping. I had disobeyed him, and he did not tolerate that. He had told me and my brothers to go get a bucket of water, but it really wasn't my turn, and my brothers left me holding the bag. I thought it was unjust, so I refused.

This particular day, when I was about ten years old, my turn came before breakfast to go fetch water to drink and cook with. We kids always took turns going down to the well because it was hard work, and we had no running water in the house. So, it being my rightful turn to do the work, I went to fetch the three gallon bucket of water from our well. It was summertime and very hot. We then spent that morning working pretty hard in the fields. When we came home for our lunch break, Dad brought the bucket into the family room, set it on the floor and said, "Boys, I need a bucket of water."

We were all in the house resting in the parlor. I remember it well, and it was Gayle's turn to get the water. Wendell and Roger went outside, and Gayle was mad at me for some reason, so he left the house too. As he left I told him, "Gayle it's your turn." What happened next will tell you something about my personality as a child growing up.

Well, I could see that bucket there, and I knew Dad would be furious if it wasn't filled. But I wasn't about to get that bucket of water. I remember getting up and walking outside and yelling from the front steps, "One of you guys better get that water," but with no results. Instead of also leaving the house, I went stubbornly back in and lay down on the couch. After about five minutes passed by the inevitable happened. Dad came in and said, "Dammit, where is my water?" I told Dad I had gotten the water that morning and it was not my turn. He said, "Lee Roy, get me a bucket of water!" He left the room and went back into the kitchen. Well, this was a real dilemma. What was I going to do?

I guess I reasoned that I had to stand up for what was right, and so I went into the kitchen to reason my plea, ending it by saying to my Dad, "What is right is right, and I am not going to get the water." I then went back and lay down on the couch.

In about a minute or two Dad came in and walked right through the family room into the yard. I cannot explain how good I felt, knowing that Dad had seen the light and was going to make Gayle get the water. I naturally got up to watch from within the house. He walked straight to one of the black locust trees, cut off a switch, and the three boys under the shade tree took notice. I remember the feeling of sorrow I had in my heart for Gayle, as I knew he was going to "get it," but my little world shattered when I noticed he was coming back toward the house.

I couldn't believe it. He was coming after me!

I got to the front porch like a light, ran around my Dad and took off for the peach trees to the south. Ironically, I was going toward the well. He took one swipe with his switch but missed as I passed and circled him. I was running as fast as I could, and he was running after me, but I outran him and ran until I was exhausted, then stopped to re-group. Now what was I going to do?

I thought all kinds of thoughts that day, from running away from home to who knows what. I know I had a lot of hate and disappointment in my heart. I finally decided to find a place to hide out, deciding on what I thought was a good place: the hopper of the combine parked at the Other Place, but man was it hot in there, exposed to the sun all afternoon.

I stayed in that sweat box until chore time and the milking was done, but the combine wasn't thirty feet from where my brothers were doing the milking, and I could overhear them talking about me, with each asking the other if they had seen me. They were saying things like, "Dad hasn't said anything about it all day," and "I feel sorry for Lee Roy when he finally comes home." I stayed there until dark, and about 9:00 p.m., after a million thoughts, decided to go home and face the music. I had made up my mind that no matter how bad a beating I might get I wasn't going to cry.

When I got home, I walked into the kitchen. No one was in sight. Everyone was in the front room or the parlor. I walked quietly upstairs and went to bed.

I never did get a whipping for that incident. I went right to sleep, so I don't know what went on or what was said when everyone else went to bed. Dad never did say anything about it, which helped soothe my heart wounds. Maybe Dad did finally see the light. I can tell you one thing for sure: everyone took their turns from that day forward when it was their turn at getting the water.

THE WHISTLE POP LESSON

When I was about twelve years old, my Dad gave me a hoe and told me to hoe some newly plowed ground so we could plant some tomatoes. I remember the soil I was hoeing was east of the cemetery at the bottom of the hill. That is the same cemetery where the Lady With The Golden Arm would come out of her grave at night looking for little boys who should be home in bed. My brothers would say, "Don't you ever go by there at night, you hear? It is hard to tell what she would do to a little boy out past bedtime!" Anyway, I think there was a culvert there just south of the ground I was hoeing, with a big cottonwood tree on the northeast edge of the plot of ground. Dad told me to come home at noon for dinner. If I got thirsty, then I could take a break and get a drink at the well, just west of the Other Place below the barn. There was a pump and a dipper there, and the water was always refreshing and cold.

Next to where I was working was a road only a few travelers traveled all day long. Some cars might pass, as well as an occasional horse and buggy, and the people would always wave to me and I of course would wave back.

After lunch – we called it dinner on the farm, since supper was the evening meal – I would go back to tilling the soil. I would go get a drink about mid-afternoon and go home close to five to do my chores and eat supper. In case you wonder how I knew what time it was, I could tell by the position of the sun. When I would hold the hoe straight up, I could tell the approximate time by where the shadow of the handle fell.

On one of the days I was hoeing this particular field, an elderly man – at least he looked old to me with his full scraggly beard – drove by with a horse and buggy on his way to the General Store to do his weekly trading. I waved and he pulled over, gesturing with his hand for me to come talk with him, and so I did. I didn't know his name, and I didn't ask. He was taking his wares, which included the eggs from his chickens and the cream he had separated from the milk from his cows, to trade for household items he might need such as flour, sugar, or beans.

He asked me who I was, and I told him I was one of the Bruner boys. He said he figured as much and asked me what I was doing. We visited for a while, and then he asked me if I was thirsty. I told him it was probably about two o'clock, and so I would take a break in about an hour and get myself a drink, pointing toward the Other Place and its well. He asked me, "If you could have anything you wished for to drink, what would it be?" I told him, "Well that's easy! A Whistle Pop!" He told me he liked Whistle Pop too.

AUTHOR'S BOTTLE OF WHISTLE POP, PHOTO BY PENNY BRUNER

I wish I could remember the man's name, but I distinctly remember him saying, "I'd better get going. Your Dad would tan my hide if he knew I was keeping you from your work." Then he drove off. I went back to my chore, keeping a watchful eye for traffic to come by and give me another excuse to lean on my hoe and wave away.

Sometime later, sure enough, I was getting thirsty, and so I held my hoe straight up and saw it was past three o'clock, and so I decided to go to the well at the Other Place to get me a drink. Having just made up my mind I looked up, and there was the old man returning down the hill toward me from the west. So I leaned on my hoe and decided to wait and watch until he passed by, and then wave away. As he approached, I did indeed wave, and again he stopped, waving me over to his buggy once again.

He asked me if I had gone for my drink yet and if I was thirsty. I told him I sure was thirsty, and I was just getting ready to go do that. He told me to climb up on his buggy, so I thought he was going to give me a short ride of two or three hundred yards to the lane at the Other Place.

When I took my seat next to him, I noticed two or three bags of groceries in the back he had traded for. There was a loaf of bread sticking out of one of the sacks, and I thought that was unusual because we never bought bread. The Bruners made homemade bread. Possibly he lived alone and didn't bake bread. He could have been a widower.

Then I looked down at the floorboard, and right there in front of me was a bucket with a little water, some ice, and two bottles of Whistle Pop! He said, "We are going to drink a Whistle Pop together!" He opened the bottles and we sat there, slowly sipping our pop and probably visiting about the weather or whatever came to our minds. While I was sipping that pop, I looked up at the old man and had a feeling come over me I can't explain. It was a good feeling, and it almost made me cry.

I had those feelings quite often growing up, and I still do as an adult. It is a generous feeling of love and kindness that speaks of God.

When we were done sharing our ice cold Whistle Pop sodas, he said he had better go. I thanked him for the treat and told him how much I appreciated it. I stood there by the side of the road for three or four minutes until he drove his buggy down the hill, past the Other Place, and then out of sight, and I remember thinking, "What a nice man he is, and when I grow up I want to be like him."

THE PARTY LINE

When I was a little boy growing up on the farm, our house was equipped with a large phone attached to the wall. It didn't have a dial with numbers on it; instead, it simply had a speaker to speak into and a hearing mechanism you placed to your ear. When we had a phone call coming in I enjoyed answering the phone.

A TYPICAL MISSOURI FARMHOUSE PHONE, CIRCA 1935

This is a picture of the phone we had in our house. My sister Georgia had the phone, but before she passed away she gave it to her son Gene, and when I was about fifty-six years old he gave it to me. He thought I should have it, since I had answered that phone a thousand times. I have so many memories concerning that phone. It is in my library at the present time.

I remember, for example, that we had a chair under the phone that I would have to stand up on to reach the receiver, or the hearing mechanism. My Dad was happy for me to answer the phone because he was usually busy with other things, and it was convenient for me. If the call was for him, then I would get the name of the person calling, yell for Dad, and, if he was within shouting distance, he would come. Many times, however, he would not be in or near the house, and then I would have to go find him. A call might sometimes be for my sisters or brothers, and I would go through the exact same process.

We did not have phone numbers back then, believe it or not; instead, we were on what was called a party line, or a telephone line shared by several families. Our party line had about eight different homes involved. Everyone on our party line had a certain ring coming from the Central Office in Civil Bend, and that ring would designate which home was to pick up the phone. Uncle Harvey's house down the road had the following ring: riiiiiing, ring (i.e., one "long" and one "short"). The Canfield's on down the road from Uncle Harvey's was riiiiiing, riiiiiing, ring (i.e., two "longs" and one "short"). The Frosts, even further down the road, was ring, ring, riiiiiing (i.e., two "shorts" and one "long"). Our ring at the Home Place was ring, ring (i.e., two "shorts"). Of course, everyone on our party line knew their own and everyone else's distinct ring.

To talk to someone on your own party line you could call them directly, not having to go through the Central Office, just by ringing their ring. Therefore, if Dad wanted to call Uncle Harvey, then he could just lift the hanging receiver, using the crank on the phone by cranking it: riiiiiing, ring. You can hardly see the crank in the picture I've provided, which is just above the writing platform on the right side of the phone. We always kept a writing pad and pencil on that platform. If you wanted to talk with anyone not on your party line, then you would simply lift the receiver and hold it to your ear. Pretty soon, either Frank or Bertie Brown would answer you, ask who you wanted to talk to, and then connect you.

Things, however, got pretty funny sometimes. For example, whenever, let's say, a sister or brother received a call from a friend at school, or heaven forbid a boyfriend might call and hope for a private conversation, and others on the party line may have "accidentally" thought your conversation might not need to be all that private, then one of the party seeking privacy would have to say, "If there is anyone else on the line would you please hang up?" Sure enough, you might then very well hear a click, then another click, as people hung up their phones. Then you might have to pause for a few more seconds and say, "Well, is there anyone else still on the line?" Then another click!

RUNNING WATER

As I mentioned earlier when discussing our garden, all the days of my life at the Home Place, from birth to leaving home after high school graduation, we never did have running water in our house. No running water to wash your hands or shave. No running water to clean your vegetables or wash your dishes. Of course, this also meant no indoor toilets. No, we had no working toilets in the house, and in fact we really had no bathrooms. All such luxuries were simply non-existent in our farmhouse in Civil Bend during that span of time.

We did have gutters on the roof of the house, and so when it would rain we would collect fresh water in a large wooden barrel we'd use for bathing, washing clothes, or other things requiring a large amount of water. We also had a large galvanized wash tub where we collected rain water. There was also a large cistern in the back porch area that was used before I was born, but I do not remember it being used when I lived on the farm.

When we bathed we used a larger, older wash pan. Bathing was a privacy issue, and before I was born my mother and older sisters would bathe in the bedroom downstairs. After I was born, my sister Ruth, sandwiched between four older brothers and four younger brothers, always bathed in the bedroom downstairs. The brothers would take their baths upstairs or in the kitchen in the wintertime or outside in the summertime by the wooden barrel.

My Dad and all the brothers shaved in the kitchen when we got old enough, using a small wash pan, and there was a mirror by the kitchen stove.

Washing dishes was done in our biggest pan in the kitchen, and we used rain water for that. Many times, however, it wouldn't rain, and then I would have to haul more buckets of water from the house well, and I didn't like that. In fact, when I got older I would carry two three-gallon buckets at a time, and that was a hard chore even for a twelve year-old boy. My oldest sister Myrtle said that when she was a child she would stand on a chair to help dry the dishes, and this was a tradition handed down to her younger sisters Georgia and Carol. I didn't start washing and drying dishes until I was about ten years old, and this is because Ruth, being the last girl living at home, assumed that chore until she became overwhelmed by all the other chores expected of women at that time: peeling potatoes, washing leaves of lettuce one by one to rid them of dirt and bugs, chopping cabbage to make slaw, cooking and all that entailed, washing and mending clothes, tending to the sick, and so on and so on. I tried to help as best I could. I also knew Ruth would eventually leave home and I would be delegated to do as many of her chores as possible. I never did learn to bake bread, though, so when Ruth left home it was Dad who baked the bread.

I'm sure that any intelligent reader will be wondering how we managed to deal with all of these situations without running water.

Let's say I came in the house from doing chores, whatever they might have been depending on how old I was, and I needed to wash my hands before breakfast. Where did I go to wash my hands and face? As I said, we had a galvanized white washing pan that sat on a table on the back porch, and I would go get it and take it to the kitchen. On top of the cook stove we kept a large tea kettle of water that was always warm, and I would pour some kettle water into the pan. I'd then return it to the back porch, where there was always a bar of homemade soap, and wash my hands and face. A towel was also there to dry my hands on. It was a community towel replaced each morning for that purpose. When several brothers had used the water in the pan, it would be thrown out in the backyard grass and replaced. We did not waste water because it was hard work to go to the well and get a three gallon bucket of water, or two, a hundred yards from the house.

When vegetables were brought from the garden that had to be washed before bringing them into the house, such as potatoes, carrots, beets, radishes, turnips, and even lettuce, we would use a bucket of water taken from the wooden barrel. Of course, it sure would have been nice if we could turn water on with a faucet in the house, but that was unknown to us.

And what it was like using the bathroom when the toilets were outside? Well, the boys could go behind the barn to pee during the day, but the girls had to use the outhouse, or the outdoor bathroom. Our outhouse was beyond our backyard in the middle of the walnut grove, about a hundred feet from the house. Inside the outhouse was a latch to lock the door to what we affectionately called the "two holer," where you sat to do your business. Worse yet, there was no such thing as toilet paper when I was a young boy, so you had to tear a sheet out of the Sears Catalog or some other magazine or newspaper. This was just the way it was. I don't know exactly when toilet paper came into being for us, but that was certainly a game changer!

Unfortunately, and as you may well imagine, a lack of toilet paper wasn't the worst of the outhouse experience. In the wintertime, day or night, if you had to use the bathroom, there would often be snow on the ground, and it was no fun trudging through the snow and ice to the outhouse. In the daytime it was bad enough, but in the nighttime it could be a nightmare. Putting on your clothes and shoes with the temperature between zero and twenty degrees was very unpleasant. In the summertime you had to contend with wasps, bees, and other nuisances. True, there was a pot to use in the bedroom if you wanted, but I hated that choice for reasons I won't go into. As a result, I learned at a very young age to go the bathroom right before I went to bed, while still fully clothed! Also, when I was very young, who wanted to go out at night with creatures such as Old One Eye and the Lady With The Golden Arm roaming about?

STOLEN COOKIES

It was nice weather, and I was seven years old. A fellow classmate and I had just finished the lunches we had brought from home, and we still had about a half hour before our afternoon classes were to begin. He asked me if I would walk down to the General Store that was only about three hundred yards from the school grounds. I told him I didn't think we should go because we weren't ever to leave the school grounds without permission. He convinced me, however, that it would be okay, and I agreed to go, even though deep down I knew we should not go.

I told him I didn't even have a penny, so I could not buy anything, but he said he didn't have any money either and we would just look around. It sounded like fun because I often went to the General Store just to look around, and Chrisy Reno didn't mind.

When we got to the store right in front were three or four bins of various cookies. Chrisy was nowhere to be seen and my classmate said the following: "I am going to get me a few cookies." And he did. He then said, "Grab a couple and let's get out of here." I took one, but I knew I was stealing and it wasn't right. Something in my heart knew I was doing something bad, but we took off with our stolen cookies.

When we got back to school my friend took a cookie out of his pocket and started eating. He told me to eat mine as well, because we couldn't go back to class with cookies in our pockets. I was reluctant, and while he finished one of his stolen cookies and was about to eat another he told me to hurry up and eat. I took one bite and gagged, and, thinking I was about to be sick, threw the cookie on the ground. Stupefied, my partner in crime said, "Stupid. What's the matter with you?" I told him I was getting sick, and he seemed okay with that. He laughed and said, "You are weird," then finished off his last stolen cookie with pleasure.

That was yet another time when growing up I realized I was not like some other kids. How could they do stuff like that and not be bothered, or at least not appear to be bothered one bit? Even today when I see grownups lie and cheat, even at games, I am amazed to think that they would rather win and destroy their character than play honestly, oftentimes losing, sometimes unfairly, and earn true character. They just don't get it, and I'm so grateful I was raised right.

I made two bad choices that day. I left school grounds without permission and I stole a cookie.

We all make bad choices in life, but deep down we know we are doing something wrong. It's true, no matter how much we convince ourselves otherwise. I guess we can't always make good choices, but when we make bad choices we should learn from them, promising to ourselves we won't make them again.

THE RADIO

When I was five and we first got electricity at the Home Place, I walked into the house when it was dark outside. I couldn't believe what I was seeing. Everything was so bright.

Dad was so proud, and the first thing he showed me was a brand new radio. He told me he had driven to Cameron that day to buy the new radio because our old one had bulbs of all kinds that always had to be replaced, and they were kind of expensive. Now, he declared, we were the proud owners of a Philco radio. It was about the size of two loaves of bread. He showed me how we could listen to different radio stations by simply turning a dial.

When I would get my chores done I was allowed to find different stations. It took me about a week to realize that I could listen to the Lone Ranger, riding his horse, named Silver, accompanied by his sidekick Tonto. I knew about the Lone Ranger because occasionally there would be a movie in Pattonsburg on Saturday night with this particular western hero in the starring role.

I loved the Lone Ranger because he was always helping people in his town. He would sometimes help a virtuous woman being harassed by some mean man who rode into town, or help some businessman being robbed by a gang of outlaws who showed up out of nowhere. Silver could sense when the Lone Ranger was in trouble. For example, the loyal horse would sense when our hero was exposed to gunfire, so he would come galloping along just in the nick of time, and the Lone Ranger would jump from some roof or other dangerous place right into Silver's saddle and miraculously get away. Tonto would then show up at just the right time and shoot the guns right out of the bad guys' hands, then tie them up and put them all in jail. Justice!

The Lone Ranger and Tonto never killed anyone, but the bad guys would always know never to come back. Bad guys with the guns shot out of their hands would be angry because their guns were ruined and their shooting hands were all bandaged up and hurt bad. Then you would see the Lone Ranger head off into the sunset, riding his loyal horse, saying, "Hi ho, Silver! Away!"

When I was listening to the radio as a young boy it was as if I was watching a movie. I would actually see everything happening in my imagination, and I think I liked it better than movies because I could create my own imaginary world every day.

There was a roll down top dresser where the radio was put, and I would get a pillow and lay down on that dresser after my chores were done, listening to programs that interested me. The Shadow was one of those programs. It was a serial about a crime fighter who had the ability to become invisible and see crimes being committed or about to be committed. The bad guys could never figure out how the police always knew about their dirty deeds. The Shadow would call the police and tell them about a crime about to be perpetrated, and they would arrive just in time to haul the criminals off to jail.

The best thing my Dad and I liked were the St. Louis Cardinal baseball games that were broadcast on the radio quite often, and we would listen together. The announcers would make the game come alive, as if we were at the game, and we hung on every pitch. In 1946, when I was ten years old, the Cardinals were in the World Series against the Boston Red Sox, with the Red Sox hero Ted Williams. We also had our hero: Stan Musial.

I would hurry home after school and catch most of the games, which were played during the day, and Dad and I would listen together outside on the back porch while working on chores nearby, such as cracking walnuts or re-pairing something. Dad was an even bigger fan of the Cardinals than I was, if such a thing is possible, and after six games the Series was tied at three games to three.

Harry Brecheen was a left-handed pitcher who was trying to win his third game of the Series for St. Louis. In the seventh inning of the seventh and decisive game, Enos Slaughter, a really good player for St. Louis, was on first base with two out, and Harry Walker got a base hit to right field. All the Red Sox players knew the Cardinals would have runners on first and third base. Slaughter, however, completely surprised the Red Sox, running right past third base and continuing toward home plate. The right fielder, being one of those Red Sox players knowing there would be runners on first and third, had nonchalantly thrown the ball to the second baseman, who then took a couple of steps and started to throw the ball to the pitcher when he realized what was going on. Panicked, he threw the ball off target and Slaughter was safe! My Dad stopped whatever he was doing and jumped up and down like a kid, and I was yelling like crazy too. Dad said, "Boy that was some play!" The game ended 4-3, with the Cardinals winning the Series. We both said we would never forget that play, and clearly I haven't.

That radio was something else, and I listened with anticipation untold times until graduating from high school. I guess you could say that the radio was the television of my life, growing up in Civil Bend.

LEAVING HOME

Before I graduated from high school, I think most of my classmates and friends, as well as most of the teachers, administrators, and adults that I knew, liked and respected me. During the graduation ceremonies the entire class was on stage. Many awards were given out that night to some of us. I gathered my share, and I felt pretty good about that. I was also the Salutatorian of the class, and so I gave a speech.

High school graduation was important stuff not only for me and my family but for the citizens of Civil Bend as well. I started school in the fall of 1941 at the age of five, and I had not yet started school when Joe Dean brought home his graduation picture, which was proudly framed to hang on the wall in the parlor along with all my other siblings' graduation pictures, joining all those who had graduated before him. All the pictures were framed in fancy glass colored frames and really looked neat. All fifteen of our pictures would eventually hang there.

When I was older, and I hung my graduation picture up there with those of my other brothers and sisters, I was especially proud that all of us had successfully completed high school. Mine was the last picture that would ever hang there. Later, when I got older, I was even more proud of Dad for seeing to it that we all shared this achievement.

Dad and Goldie were there for my Salutatorian speech, and so was my brother Miles, now returned from the war for some time, and his wife Kay, who was a grade school teacher. All of the faculty and all of the school board members were there, including Harold Munn, the school board President, who was a good friend of Miles. Mr. Munn was the one who gave me and all the seniors our graduation diplomas.

When Mr. Munn gave me my diploma, he congratulated me and shook my hand, asking what my plans were. I told him I was going to work for my brother Homer in his restaurant the coming summer and then go to college to become a pharmacist. He sincerely wished me luck, adding that if there was anything he could do for me when I got out of college to come and see him, and he would see what he could do.

Four college years passed and I managed to take my degree. I was 21 years old and wanted to get my own pharmacy as soon as I could, but it was going to take a little time to save enough money to accomplish that dream. Then I remembered Mr. Munn and what he had said to me. Miles had purchased a farm next to Dad's farm and was living nearby, and I told him what his friend

Harold Munn had said. I also told him I was going to ask Mr. Munn if he would loan me the money to purchase a store I had found. Miles said that Mr. Munn had asked about me, and about how I was coming along with my education a year or so back, so I should go ahead and talk to him.

I drove over to his house in my brand new 1957 Chevy – that car turned out to be a classic – and knocked on his door. He recognized me and asked me in, wanting to know what was on my mind. I told him, and he agreed. I was to pay him 8% interest, and he asked to have the loan paid off in five years if at all possible. I told him I was pretty sure I could do that, and then I went on to pay the loan off in three years. We were both happy about that. When I drove to his house and made the final yearly payment I thanked him, and I told him I would always be grateful that he helped me get off to a good start with my career. I still feel that way today.

The drug store I bought on the first day of 1959 was in Greenfield, Missouri, in the southwest corner of the state. I lived there for about six years and then moved on, eventually owning four pharmacies at one time. They were all within a fifty mile radius: Greenfield, Seymour, Mansfield, and Willard. I sold three of them eventually, ending up in Willard for thirty-two years, after which I sold that pharmacy to my nephew, John Bruner, Gayle's son, on the first day of 2005.

I am married to a wonderful woman, Vivian, and we have raised three wonderful children, Michael, Lori, and Penny, who all graduated from Willard High School and later college with many honors and degrees of their own, and Vivian graduated from college as well. Thanks again, Harold Munn, for helping me get my wonderful life started.

Let me leave you with a final Dad story, which is an up.

When I was about twenty years old, and I know it was in that time frame, I called Dad from Kansas City one weekend and told him I was driving up to see him and Goldie. I told him I would be coming up Friday after work, that I would be late, and not to wait up for me. I would see them both on Saturday morning.

I got there about 11:00 p.m. and Dad was waiting up for me. He had a deck of cards in his hands and asked if I wanted to play. We played for a while and visited, and about midnight I told him we had better get to bed because there would be some chores to do before breakfast: perhaps not as many as there used to be, but he was still milking a couple of cows. Then I thanked him for staying up.

THE HOME PLACE, CIRCA 1974

I was about to tell Dad something he had never heard from me before. It took some courage, but if you knew my Dad you would understand. Dad was not a lovey, let's hug type of guy. He didn't hug or show affection. He was tough, stern, and honorable, but I really could not remember him ever telling me he loved me, nor I him. I just told him there was something I wanted to tell him, and for the first time in my life I told him that I loved him.

It took him by surprise, and he told me he loved me too, for the first time in his life, then all of a sudden he burst into tears, uncontrollably crying. This went on for over a minute, and I was tearing up too. He said to me, "I'm sorry for being such a terrible father."

I could not believe he said that.

I told him, "That's not true!" I said, "How many children did you raise? I believe if I counted right it was fifteen, wasn't it"? He said, "Yes." I said, "How many do you think know right from wrong?" He said, "All of them I hope." I said, "Of course they do. How many of us finished high school? All of us did. Several of us have gone on to college. One became a dentist, one a veterinarian, three are pharmacists. One got a degree in political science, one a degree in counseling. Many served, three fought, and two died defending the freedom of this country that you love! How many of us were taught to work hard, be honest, and become useful citizens? How many of us went to prison for some crime? Come on Dad, you had a tough road to hoe. You had a lot of downs. Don't ever believe you were not a good Dad!"

I gave him a big hug, and he returned the favor, and once again I felt the presence of God. That was one of the greatest moments of my life, and I bet it was for him too.

BRUNER/HENDERSON GENERAL STORE IN CIVIL BEND, MO 1892

GENERAL STORE IN CIVIL BEND WEEKS BEFORE ITS DESTRUCTION

COLOPHON

Stories of Civil Bend was designed & typeset by Bill Roberts at Bottle of Smoke Press in North Salem, New York. The text is set in Goudy Old Style.

The first edition was published by Rose of Sharon Press and limited to one hundred paperback copies & forty hardcover copies.

This second edition was published in September 2021.

GEORGE HAVER

JAMES HAVER

JOHN

OTHNEIL BRU

JOSEP

JOHN RECK

HARVEY HAVER

VER

MINNIE HAVER

ER, SR.

OTHNIEL BRUNER, JR.

HAVER
VIRGIL
PAUL
RUSSELL

RUSSELL BRUNER

FANNIE RECK

RECK

MYRTLE
VERN
OLEN
GEORGIA
HOMER
LOWELL
CAROL
MILES
JOE DEAN
JOHNNY
RUTH
WENDELL
ROGER
GAYLE
LEE ROY

www.ingramcontent.com/pod-product-compliance
Lightning Source LLC
Chambersburg PA
CBHW060052100426
42742CB00014B/2800